AF511970

NEPAL INTERTWINED with INDIA-CHINA INTEREST

NEPAL INTERTWINED with INDIA-CHINA INTEREST

Author

Umesh K. Bhattarai

ADROIT

Adroit Publishers

NEW DELHI • KATHMANDU

ISBN : 978-81-87393-79-5

2020

Copyright © : Author

No part of this publication may be reproduced or transmitted in any form or by any means, electronic or mechanical, including photocopying, recording or any information storage and retrieval system, without permission in writing from the publisher & author.

Published by
ADROIT PUBLISHERS 4675/21, Ganpati Bhawan, Ansari Road,
Daryaganj, New Delhi-110 002 Phone : 011-23266030
adroitpublishers@gmail.com
C/O Vajra books, Thamel, Jyatha,
Kathmandu, Nepal l KTM: +977-9808357451

Typeset in Garamond Premier Pro by Arun, Akriti Graphic
Solution, Delhi-110081 E-mail: arun263923@gmail.com,
Ph: 9999414390

Contents

Abstract

Nepal Intertwined with India-China Interest is an empirical study that identifies potential threats to Nepal from its neighbours and other power centres. The socio-politico-economic condition of Nepal has been messed due to diverged interest of different groups, tribes and ethnicity. The caste system had created a vacuum and prevented the providing of an equal opportunity to all. The deprived and marginalized groups were humiliated by the systems. Such systems were blindly supported by the colonial power under the British rule in India favouring autocratic rulers who promised to meet its interest. The British East India Company and later, the Union of India had an eye on Nepal's resources. For this, they trapped Nepal's *durbar* under their grip to weaken its nationalism so that no popular resentment occurred.

On the other hand, China had little intake to interfere in Nepal's politics as the Himalayas was the natural barrier in the past. But now, the situation is changing. In fact, it has major interest to protect Tibet from the outside world. Tibet has remained a centre of gravity for the westerns to weaken China through Nepal. For instance, Nepal had to mobilize its army against the US trained Khampa rebels fighting against the Chinese rule in Tibet. China still perceives the "US Indo-Pacific Strategy" is guided against it. On the one side, the ruling Nepal Communist Party looks like it is under pressure to become its member, and on the other side—the US claim of Nepal as a full-fledged member to this strategy has confused scholars in Nepal. Nevertheless, Nepal has already signed the "Belt and Road Initiative" of China on which it is suspicious to fall into a debt trap in the manner in which Sri Lanka and others are victimized.

The way Nepal is moving towards fragility, it must correct its position in the international power dynamics. It must revise the old treaties that it has signed with the neighbours first and others next. After President Xi Jinpin's visit to

Nepal on October 12, 2019, there is a turn in Nepal's policy. How the legislative body will ratify the treaties and the moves of the Nepal Government - time will tell us. Similarly, India also seems to be thinking to renew the Indo-Nepal relations in the changed perspective. The voice has been heard from various articles published from New Delhi recently. The US Embassy in Kathmandu has also been noticed trying to convice the Nepal Government to accept support under the Millenium Challenge Corporation (MCC) to Nepal. This is said to be part of the Indo-Pacific Strategy. If so, how will it move? We need to wait for some time. But in either way, the democratic process must be followed through consensus in the parliament. The diverged power centres must be brought into a single grid and only a vibrant public diplomacy can make it possible. The other entities that can support a nation are its public institutions. In a fragile state, they are weak—so the endeavour should be to revive them.

As a matter of fact, in any nation an army is formed and a system is developed to integrate as well as to protect itself from the internal as well as the external threats. King Prithvi Narayan Shah, the founder of the Nepali nation, did this for its integration. Although military history of Nepal can be traced from 350 BCE, the Lichchhabi king Narendra Dev had a bigger standing army that provided support by sending a credible number of cavalry and infantry force to China, to invade the southern kingdoms in CE 647. Later on, other than King Pratap Malla, the Malla rulers who succeeded the Lichchhabi could not retain similar powers as they were divided into many small principalities.

In the late medieval period, colonial powers like Britain, France, Spain, Netherlands and Portugal invaded the entire world, including South and South East Asia. After the 17th century, when many tiny states and principalities were quarrelling among themselves, and were not really aware of the British move for trading in this part of the world, the visionary King Prithvi Narayan Shah understood the trend and determined to unify Nepal to counter the British invasion.

With slow success initially, he could expand Nepal eastward but could not complete the westward movement due to his untimely death at the age of 51 in 1775. The westward expansion was completed by his son Bahadur Shah, defeating all the Baise and the Choubise principalities, including Kumao, Garhwal and up to the Satluj River. To keep Nepal intact, King Prithvi Narayan Shah and his successors fought many battles with the British East India Company, Tibet and

China. *Dibya Upadesh* by King Prithvi Narayan Shah envisions many aspects, including the geostrategic importance of Nepal to balance powers from Central Asia to South Asia.

The Nepal Army was instrumental throughout Nepal's expansionary period in keeping its territory intact after the 1816 Treaty with the British. Nepal's military history coincides with the country's history as well, because the rulers used the military as the only tool to prolong their regime. The rulers after Prithvi Narayan Shah and Bahadur Shah were neither innovative nor creative to administer conquered territory as a nation. The British quickly recognised the problems of those areas and the qualities of the youth, and hence opted to recruit them in their army, as did King Ranjit Singh of Punjab.

Prime Minister Jung Bahadur understood the recruitment dilemma, so he was reservist to some extent. But considering the geopolitical situation of the country, he compromised his policy to suit the broader British interest in the region. His military support to quell the Sepoy Mutiny in India was perhaps inspired by his wish to remain in power through the blessings of the British and get some of the territory Nepal had lost after the Sugauli Treaty. He succeeded in the latter objective by getting the British to agree to return Banke, Bardiya, Kailali and Kanchanpur after 45 years of its occupation in 1860.

The Nepal Army's contribution to nation-building throughout its existence has been commendable, but autocratic rulers have misused it at times. The rule of Bhimsen Thapa and the way he emerged into power is not only controversial; the army was also blamed for terrorising the opponents. It is even questioned whether he was really a patriot or was merely hungry for power. He discredited the army's image in history. Jung Bahadur also emerged to power like Bhimsen Thapa from the Kot massacre in 1846. In retrieving territory lost to the British, he tried to save face.

It was not only Thapa and Rana rulers who misused the army to fulfil their ambition, but the Shah kings and their regent queens also misused it. King Rana Bahadur Shah ruled whimsically, as personalities like Bhimsen Thapa and Pandit Rang Nath advised. The regent Queen Rajendra Laxmi, who had the attorney power from her husband King Rajendra Bikram, misused military power through Jung Bahadur and Gagan Singh Bhandari.

From 1743, when the Nepali Army was founded – in 274 years of its history, it was left on the disposal of the Shah rulers at times to de facto powers like Bhimsen Thapa, Jung Bahadur and many more on the other side. In the process of democratic transition, it was also employed to crush insurgency. The justification for this may be debatable, but the army was always loyal to the regime, which was formed by popular mandate. In 1960, King Mahendra imposed an emergency and arrested the democratically elected Prime Minister B. P. Koirala and his cabinet members. Likewise, after 1990, the democratically elected prime ministers also resigned over the issue of civil supremacy when Girija Prasad Koirala failed to mobilise the army against the Maoist insurgency and Puspa Kamal Dahal dismissed General Rookmangad Katawal as well. In a nutshell, the imposition of an impartial rule of law is the only means to keep both the military as well as the civil society on track through empowered public institutions.

In order to carry out an empirical research, the entire work is focused to review Nepal's history, the pros and cons of its creation as a modern state, restoration of democracy in a new federal democratic republican model and the political wrangling to manage the Nepal Army in its early democratic set-up. The way public institutions are losing their ground to support it from the grassroots, Nepal is slow to recover from the fragility that it has been facing from decades long Maoist insurgency and a prolonged transition thereafter. Although the ruling communist government is trying to re-establish the damaged institutions and reconstruct the nation, its dictatorial autocratic behaviour is creating a rift and confusion among the liberal segments of the society. And the reason is solely due to its inept, incompetent, and short-sighted leaders. They speak much and promise high but the delivery of public goods and services is poor. If the political leaders do not improve themselves, it would no longer be a surprise for Nepal to turn into a problem. The impact is gradually noticed in the foreign policy failure, which is obviousely an extension of the domestic policies which are not strong enough to support the national interest at large. The book reveals more into it.

In addition, the international power centres play through proxies to weaken its poor political institutions to fulfill their vested interest. The poor socio-economic condition is misused by such powers as the country's geopolitics is favourable if used against its neighbours. In such milieu, the power play will continue against this weakening of its institutions more rapidly, hence the threat to their stability will increase. The proxies are now mainly used in the social sectors to erode their religious and cultural values. The spread of Christianities and Islamic ideologies in the Hindu and the Buddhist dominated areas in Nepal and in North India as well as in the Buddhist and the Han community in China are the burning examples.

Umesh K. Bhattarai

Acknowledgements

The main objective of this book *Nepal Intertwined with India-China Interest* is to acquaint the readers on the pros and cons of the trilateral interests prevailing among Nepal, India and China from the past to the present. The history is the witness as to how our ancesters managed the various powers to keep Nepal intact when both the north and the south of Nepal fell into the hands of the imperials of that time. It was never under the colonial rule but rather it tried hard to maintain its independence, sovereignty and freedom intact. But now, Nepal is becoming weaker day by day because of its own mismanaged domestic policies, lack of will power in mainstream leaders to deal against corruption as well as rampant law and order situation.

Being a buffer to two burgeoning economies of the world, Nepal is still not able to utilize such opportunies due to the lack of proper vision and will power to development. Corruption is the main hurdle as it is entrenched deep into its culture as well as tradition. Unless the cultural transformation against corruption takes place – nothing is going to change in present political order. In addition, this book also analyses its neighbour's interests in Nepal from the time of its inception as a state. As Nepal was integrated from various small principalities, Nepal Army's role to unite was commendable. At times, the history of Nepal coincides with the military history as well. So, we must bear into our mind that they are synonym to each other. Because of this reason, most Nepalies take pride in the Nepal Army as an institution.

In order to promote national interest, the role of Nepal Army has been considered important all the time. There are lots of evidences in the Nepali history where the politics was saved from falling into selfish hands—from people who have tried to isolate the institution to fulfil their vested interest, which resulted into further plunging into the deep problem. Keeping all of these into consideration, the book focuses on issues of national interests as well as on the aspirations and the wishes of the international powers on it.

In order to gather informations, facts and figures; the renouned personalities like the former Vice-Chancellor and historian Prof. Dr. Triratna Manandhar, Lumbini Buddhist University, Prof. Dinesh Raj Pant, Mahendra Sanskrit University and Nepal Academy, Mr. Gagan Raj Bhatta, a close ally and a Nepali Congress co-partner of former Prime Minister Dr. K. I. Singh and the then Nepal Army Spokesperson Brig. Gen. Tara Bahadur Karki helped to rendering of their opinions and views through interviews and questionnaires. Likewise, I am indebted to Dr. Ganga Prasad Acharya and Mrs. Reema Acharya and my beloved wife Mrs. Neel Bhattarai, daughters Roshani, Prativa, Pratigya and son Pragyan for their ceaseless support in my endeavour. Similarly, I extend my gratitude to Suraj, Prajjwal, and Amit as well as Editor Ms. Gracy Samjetsabam and overall, Mr. Akhil Sharma from Adroit Publishers, New Delhi for publishing the book in such a short period of time.

December 03, 2019 **Umesh K. Bhattarai**

List of Boxes

Abbreviations/Acronyms

BBIN	:	Bangladesh, Bhutan, India and Nepal
BCE	:	Before the Common Era
BCIM	:	Bangladesh, China, India and Myanmar
BIMSTEC	:	Bay of Bengal Initiative for Multi-Sectoral and Economic Cooperation
BF	:	Bingfa (Art of War)
BRI	:	Belt and Road Initiative
BRICS	:	Brazil, Russia, India, China, South Africa
CA	:	Constituent Assembly
CE	:	Common Era
CIAA	:	Commission for Investigation of Abuse of Authority
COAS	:	Chief of the Army Staff
CPEC	:	China-Pakistan Economic Corridor
DDR	:	Disarmament, Demobilization and Reintegration
EPG	:	Eminent Persons Group
FDI	:	Foreign Direct Investment
HLPC	:	High Level Political Committee
IDP	:	Internally Displaced People
MEA	:	Ministry of External Affairs
NA	:	Nepal Army
NC	:	Nepali Congress
NCP	:	Nepal Communist Party
NSC	:	National Security Council
OBOR	:	One Belt One Road
QSD	:	Quadrilateral Security Dialogue
RPP	:	Rastriya Prajatantra Party
SAARC	:	South Asian Association for Regional Cooperation

SC	:	Supreme Court
SCO	:	Shanghai Cooperation Organization
UML	:	United Marxist Lenninist
UN	:	United Nations
YCL	:	Young Communist League

Chapter One

Introduction

Conceptual Analysis

A state is formed, organised and strengthened to promote national interest by stabilising the entire system conducive to national development. For this, the core national values need to be identified. The national interest should be defined, politically debated and approved. "National security strategy" should follow it as policy doctrine for modern nationhood. In the case of Nepal, have these procedures been followed? Of course, not in the way this philosophy is understood in today's democratic setup. This may be a reason why Nepal regularly plunges into both domestic upheavals and foreign policy lapses.

Nepal's nationhood was developed in an autocratic setup. The ruling class presumed the whole nation as its private property and the people merely as a resource to serve at its disposal. After King Prithvi Narayan Shah's death, his successors forgot his *Dibya Upadesh,* that envisaged the people as the source of power and the entire state mechanism dedicated to serve the people. They considered people merely as peasants rather than stakeholders of the nation. In Nepal's early history, the de-facto rulers like Bhimsen Thapa, Jung Bahadur Rana and his brothers under the regency of the Shah dynasty deprived the people through military might.

There were five leading families contending for power during Thapa's period—the Shah, the Choutariya, the Basnyat, the Pandey and the Thapa. The working for these families and their factions were hill Brahmins who acted as preceptors, astrologers and Newars that occupied the secondary administrative positions. If a family or faction achieved power, they killed—exiled or demoted members of the opposing alliance. Senior military ranks were filled by the ruling family and used as a means to terrorise opponents. The Nepal Army was considered to be family-centric from its inception.

Bhimsen Thapa as the first outsider could garner military support for his objectives. He modernised the army on the French model. He had an antipathy for the British while he accompanied King Rana Bahadur on an asylum at Banaras in India. French engineers were employed to build modern arms and equipment, including cannon for the Nepal Army during his premiership.[1] Thapa was a close ally of King Rana Bahadur, who was killed by his step-brother. It is suspected that the plot was hatched by Thapa himself. The second outsider de-facto ruler was Jung Bahadur Rana, who came to power through the Kot massacre with the support of "Bijuli Garat," a core military group under his command. Then onwards, the Nepali leadership was influenced by the military to reach power and rule the people.

Nepal's geopolitical location also compelled the country to take care in the manner it deals with the regimes of its two giant neighbours in the south and in the north. Bhimsen Thapa failed in his endeavour to retain greater Nepal and was compelled to sign the 1816 Treaty with the East India Company, which confined his dominion to Nepal's present boundary. But Jung Bahadur Rana managed to please the British by providing them military support, both lawful and unlawful. In return, he regained the lost territory of Banke, Bardiya, Kailali and Kanchanpur from the British in 1860.[2]

Although we talk much about civil supremacy in the democratic setup of a small and buffer country like Nepal, democracy itself is costly for a society that is closed and traditional. An undeveloped and poorly structured society with a multi-ethnic character generally lacks cohesion. But trust, social harmony and assimilation even in a divergent society can be achieved if the leaders have vision, a spirit of sacrifice and dedication to democracy and inclusion. South Africa and its leader Nelson Mandela can be taken as an example in this regard.

The Nepal Army has never been a problem in promoting democracy. As it has been attached for long with a single ruling family as its patron, it requires some time to transform itself. Harmonious civil-military relations is must for Nepal's stability due to its geopolitical location, poor economic condition and divergent social structure. According to Tri Ratna Manadhar, both in 1950 and 1960 (the First Revolution of Nepal and when King Mahendra assumed absolute power from the people's elected government), the army worked for the

1. Acharya, Baburam, *General Bhimsen Thapa: Yini lai maile jasto dekhe,* Srikrishna Acharya, 2008, p. 34.
2. Bhattarai, Umesh K., "Madhesi Agitation: Comprehending Consequences on Indo-Nepal Relations", *The Diplomatist*, November 2015.

government in power. On both the occasions, when the government changed, the army became loyal to the successor government.[3]

Security is a prerequisite for a nation's sustainable development. The decades-long Maoist rebellion and the legacy of autocratic rule weakened the state's capacity to ensure human security. Although the transition after the Maoist rebellion is long and also embroiled with clear cut functional line between the federal, the province and the local governments—there is still an opportunity to have political transformation from an autocracy to a democracy and the restructuring of the security sector so as to protect the foundation of democracy and run the country as per its norms.[4] These are the theoretical aspects. But in practical life, it is difficult to apply these theories unless the mindset is changed. We commonly try to change others but fail to change ourselves. We listen to our heart and ignore the mind, which represents wisdom and justice. Most leaders in Nepal have failed due to this trait.

Security Phenomena

The Cold War era brought forth many key issues that forced nation-states to pay a high cost for national security. Even after the end of the Cold War, many developing countries were trapped in civil wars and insurgencies.[5] This was due to divergent interests prevailing over national security interests. A nation cannot alone decide how the power centres play against its national interest. The geopolitics of a nation is a major factor that dictates its challenges and the opportunities. The national capacity to use its geopolitics as strength depends on its intellectual capital. Loyalty and honesty of such intellectual capital is important for a nation to flourish.

The other key issues emerging in our political spectrum are comprehensive partnership, strategic interaction and global strategic stability. These phenomenons have been identified recently by Chinese President Xi Jinping during his visit to Russia to meet President Vladimir Putin as necessity to deal with all the elements of international diplomacy. Of course, they are important to

3. Tri Ratna Manadhar, the former Vice Chancellor of Lumbini Buddhist University, is a renowned historian of Nepal. He made this comment in response to a questionnaire regarding the Nepal Army's role in strengthening democracy and ensuring the people's rights.
4. Bhattarai, Baburam, "Nepali Rajniti Ko Bhabi Disha", *Kantipur Daily*, 24 March 2010.
5. Thapa, Karna Bahadur, "National Security of Nepal 1990-2000: A Study of Concept, Vulnerabilities and Threats", Dissertation, Kathmandu, Tribhuvan University, 2002 (unpublished).

determine the evolutionary dynamism to develop a rule to enhance international connectivity in the present world order. To safeguarding the multilateralism, we must follow the principle of global strategic stability through strategic interaction within the comprehensive partnership in our neighbourhood specifically. In gist, we must be more than a partner but less than an ally to keep our relations vibrant.[6] Perhaps, this could be the reason for President Xi Jinping's identifying it in the latest visit to Nepal as "strategic partner" for development through the joint communiqué published in Kathmandu.

The above identifications by the world leaders are really important for the countries like Nepal which is located in a sensitive position from the geopolitical perspective. Irrespective of size, it is strategically important to balancing relations between two giants of Asia that is India and China. The comprehensive partnership that one of its neighbours raised has deep meaning in international politics. As development requires multi-dimensional approach to achieve, a country may need multiple partnerships to implement mega projects that have international value in global economics. Such projects need huge foreign direct investments (FDI) that country like Nepal cannot manage from internal resources. The way the Nepali economics and governance model are moving today, it will be impossible to attract FDI unless the "rule of law" is précised and law enforcement agencies are determined. President Xi Jinping's first identification of "comprehensive partnership" for Nepal will only be effective if it understands how it can attract FDI through vibrant rule of law and effective governance with zero-tolerance on corruption.

To define strategic interaction from Nepali perspective, it has a long way to go to determine the evolutionary dynamism to develop a rule for comprehensive partnership in the present world order. As the political culture is ruined badly, promoting multilateralism in the present Nepali politics is very easy. The overplay in the internal politics by the international power centres has reduced the capacity of the national entity to take decisive actions essential to balance global vis-à-vis regional strategic stability. So, understanding to be more than a partner and be less than an ally has no meaning to the present political leaders who have no vision to interact strategically with their international counterparts in the global international politics.

6. Bashu Mishra's post in FaceBook shared by Kul Bahadur Khadka on June 18, 2019.

Unless Nepal develops a culture for research and development in strategic studies, it will remain poor in balancing its activities in the global vis-à-vis the regional strategic stability. Strategic interaction through vibrant think tank is the only way to develop a vision and garner opinions of the like-minded intellectuals for a consensus on the contentious issues. The present political leadership must encourage a culture to listen to the opinions of the scholars in the matters of global strategic stability before they interact to developing comprehensive partnership in global issues. Understanding President Xi's view points and interpreting it for our own benefit require a high degree of intellectuality.

In fact, we must understand that stability of Nepal will not prevail unless all the aforementioned activities are made conducive to promote national integration directed to increase awareness on common identity amongst the citizens of a country. It is an emotional attachment as well as the sense of common belonging of the nationalism irrespective of caste, class, religion, ethnicity and language. Unity in diversity comes at the foremost when the nation is in a crisis like war or other calamities. It is the fusion of nationalism and patriotism synthesised through cohesiveness that is mapped in terms of unified integration. Extremism once radicalised negates social harmony either as ultra-nationalism or ultra-anti-nationalism. Both are destructive for national integration.

National security denotes an effort by the apparatus of national power to ensure the protection, persuasion and preservation of defined national interest. The latter can further be subdivided into "vital national interest and important national interest". Vital national interest may be to ensure a nation's territorial integrity, national freedom of action, sovereignty, and national unity. The first step towards national security is for the state to define its vital national interest. The second step is to identify immediate and long-term threats to the national interest. In the third step, the state should create adequate ways and means to face these threats. Likewise, important national interests may be to protect the lives of citizens, to work on poverty alleviation and economic development, preservation of natural resources, to promote international peace and security, to enhance environmental conservation, to bring political stability, to secure religious harmony, to protect of human rights and to ensure human security.

Are these national interests protected in Nepal? Per se, the autocratic rulers of the country defined national interests, whimsically. The monarchy created its own institutions which were above the law. The national anthem was all about the monarchical power, which also symbolised national unity and sovereignty. The military was at the monarch's disposal and security analysis was the responsibility of his Principal Military Secretariat at the palace.

The second popular unrest of 1990, however, forced the king to become the constitutional head and restore the multi-party system for the second time in Nepal's history. The new constitution envisaged a National Security Council (NSC) but its composition was faulty. The Prime Minister was its chair and the Defence Minister and the Chief of the Army Staff (COAS) were its members. Most of the time, the defence portfolio was held by the Prime Minister himself. Prime Minister Girija Prasad Koirala wanted to move the army against the Maoists in 2000, but the then COAS, General Prajwalla Shumser Rana rejected his proposal. The Prime Minister then appointed Mahesh Acharya as the Defence Minister to complete the quorum. But later, when the palace rejected the proposal, Prime Minister Koirala resigned.

There is a prolonged debate in Nepal, as to whether the national security is the only concern of the government or the civil society and the professional experts should also be included in the NSC. Late Dr Madhukar Rana, a leading intellectual and a former finance minister, opined that security in Nepal had been compromised due to the traditional stranglehold of the palace and Military Secretariat, the Army's inability to mobilise public opinion with effective public relations, and the utter lack of a harmonious interface among the various security agencies. The new constitution has removed some of the drawbacks, but the NSC is still like the defence council as before.

The new constitution includes some ministers like the home minister, the finance minister and the foreign affairs as well as a Chief Secretary and a COAS as the members of the NSC, but excludes the information and technology minister even though it has an important role to play in the national as well as the international security.[7] But interestingly, there is no provision for a National Security Adviser. Lacking such an appointment, the institution becomes directionless. The coordinator's responsibility has been given to the Defence Secretary, who is not an expert in this sector.

Overall, in the NSC there is only one single security expert that is the COAS. Most of the lawmakers ignore the fact that the national security strategy is an art as well as a science to employ the nation's intellectual, political, economic,

7. Constitution of Nepal 2015, Part 28, Provisions Relating to National Security.

informational and military power to achieve national security objectives, which lacks in Nepal's NSC. In the monarchical period, all deficiencies were blamed to the autocratic rule. But in the current democratic dispensation as well, we are facing the same problem of leaders being short-sighted, non-visionary, self-styled and selfish.

To understand the national problem, we must understand the intertwined regional issues into it. At times, it may have links with global concerns. India-China enjoys tremendous economic growth and the USA plays a critical part in the emergence of these two major powers in Asia. In 2006, it was expected that the US relations with India will continue to check China's influence in Asia, but it did not happen so. India categorically dismissed suggestions as their country should be part of any US containment strategy towards China and had cited the importance of booming economic ties with it.[8] Although both the officials in New Delhi and Washington have stressed that as both being "natural" partner traditionally and have multi-ethnic democracies at large, but geographically the USA is in far distance compared to China which has common borders with it.

India-China relations are also not as cordial as we think they are. They have border disputes in their entire northern front but still they share common positions in many international issues. Their bilateral trade has reached to US $ 89.6 billion in 2017-18 with total trade deficit widening to altogether US $ 62.9 billion in Chinese favour. Besides, the trade volume is expected to reach US $ 100 billion in few years.

Although meetings of high-level delegates have increased in recent years, they contradict to each other wherever their national interest clashes. But there are few examples where their interest converges, they tend to even override the right of others. The Lipulek area is one example which is encroached for India-China transit in western Nepal. But still, the recent visit of a high-level Chinese delegate in Nepal has enabled a paradigm shift in the overall relations not only with China as a "strategic partner" for development but also, it challenged India to improve its relations with Nepal from a totally new perspective.

Contradictions after Xi's Visit in Nepal

President Xi Jinpings' latest visit of Nepal on October 12, 2019 has raised concerns on the dynamics of Nepal's relations with China and India. Some expect

8. https://www.cfr.org/backgrounder/india-china-and-united-states-delicate-balance

the impact of the visit as new discourse on alleged loosing Indian hegemony over Nepal. In fact, the Indian intelligentsia have over emphasized the "geopolitical" constraints of Nepal as major hurdles not only to its development but also the compulsion to keep entire relations confine to its southern neighbour. The fabricated "geopolitical" phobia that was much hiked in cold war era has been now dismantled once President Xi assured to make Nepal "land-linked" from "land-locked".

There was the time when China used to prescribe Nepal to be close with India for its development but now the situation has changed. It is more assertive to its policy on connectivity and keen to join Nepal into it for development and prosperity. The joint communiqué published after President Xi's visit to grade Nepal as a "strategic partner" has deep meaning in international politics. C. Raja Mohan in his recent article published in *The Indian Express* revealed that there are three options left to Nepal to craft its strategy and based on those India-Nepal relations should be developed.[9] Firstly, neutrality and symmetry need to be balanced in its relations. For this, he categorically mentioned King Birendra's "peace zone proposal" after several years which was not welcomed by the then government, need to be pursuied separately. Secondly, either to establish special relationship with China alone or thirdly, continue a dynamic balancing and make the best of the possibilities with both India and China.

He hinted as if Nepal adopted status quo—it has to turn its open border with India into a closed one similar to the northern frontier with China. If Nepal's strategic tilt towards China, it would mean Kathmandu would want to discard the special privilege it has in the relationship with Delhi, for example, the freedom for Nepali citizens to live and work in India. Here C. Raja Mohan missed out to mention what Nepal has given to India (see, Gorkha Recruitment and Jung Bahadur in subsequent chapters). Nevertheless, he emphasized that the protectorate relationship that Delhi inherited from the British Raj was never sustainable. So, it must own its share of strategic error in dealing with Nepal.

For this, he suggested a correction measure for Delhi to offer a new pact with Nepal that can build on the mutual geographic and cultural interdependence

---

9. C. Raja Mohan. China's dramatic rise in the 21st century makes Beijing a far more compelling partner for Kathmandu, The Indian Express, October 22, 2019.

   https://indianexpress.com/article/opinion/columns/xi-jinping-nepal-visit-narendra-modi-xi-summit-india-nepal-relations-6080914/?fbclid=IwAR1rJXem164ryQ3La5IsQW24_cknT0K9YXDiiNpFRqGOUL9V1RTSA73Fhwk (Accessed on October 25. 2019.

between the two countries. Here, he again missed out to mention the pending Eminent Persons Groups' recommendations which both the countries' governments i.e. Modi and Oli had formed to suggest on the ways and means to improve bilateral relations within the framework of India-Nepal Friendship Treaty 1950. In fact, it was Delhi's reluctance to response Nepal's voice from the very beginning.

Whenever Indo-Nepal relations were strained, Delhi opted punitive action of embargo to tame Nepal's elites but ignored the main sufferer who were the poor Nepalis. Now, it is that group who voted unanimously for the Oli led party to form the government that is blamed for having strategic tilt towards China. As a result, Nepal turned to the northern front to break its "land-locked" geopolitics into "land-linked" geostrategic manoeuvre and nothing else.

Impact of Nepal's Fragility to Neighbours

The open border with India will have negative impact if Nepal's fragility rises. Despite of huge presence of para-military forces at the border, the socio-economic spillover cannot be fully controlled. We have noticed such activities during the economic embargo imposed by India and movement of Internally Displaced People (IDP) at the time of Maoist insurgency in Nepal. On the contrary, the case of the Bhutanese Nepali refugees and long-term residing Nepali origin Assamese pushed forcefully by the Indian establishment into the Nepali territory were different. If socio-economic unrest takes place, such migration may be volunteer of Medhesi and other Nepalis having relations with Indian nationals if Nepal falls in turmoil.

The way Westerners are spreading Christianity and the gulf countries are supporting Muslims to spread Islamic ideology in Nepal may have impacts even towards North India— and there is the possibility of Hindus and Buddhists gearing up against religious conversion. The way Islam is spreading its ideology through Madarsa's in support of like-minded Islamic states may rise up tension at the borders. Although religion conversion is banned by the Constitution of Nepal, the missionaries and the Madarsa's are defying legal provision because the Government of Nepal is unable to restore rule of law in the country.

The case is becoming further complicated when the US Department of State declared on its 2018 Report that Nepal is a "secular state" but defined secularism as to "protection of the age-old religion and culture". It blames as the constitution prohibits conversion from one religion to another and bans religious behaviour disturbing public order or contrary to public health, decency and morality.[10] The report commented critically on Nepal's anti-conversion policy, when it formalized its new criminal code which became effective in August 2018 reducing the punishment for converting the religion of another person from six to five years imprisonment. The report also highlighted the Government of Nepal's weakness to protect the small religious groups which includes discussions concerning access to burial grounds, public celebration of religious holidays, prohibition against conversion and verbal attacks on Christian communities by Hindu politicians.

At the other, India in the second innings of Mr. Narendra Modi as prime-minister is likely to show new vision and approach to protect Hinduism in the region. The formation of his new cabinet of ministers indicates enough as what sort of policy he may adopt this time. His close ally and Chief Minister of Uttar Pradesh Yogi Aditya Nath had already revealed his intension in 2016 in a speech to World Hindu Conference in Kathmandu.[11] He is a die heart supporter of monarchy and Hinduism in Nepal. The way Prime Minister Modi had taken against the secularism at the eve of Nepal's constitution promulgamation in 2015 is a burning example of his support for Hinduism. In the changed scenario, one can easily predict how the political situation will be in this part of the world.

Similarly, China is also forming a community of its own in the Sino-Nepal border area so that it can keep an eye on Nepal and other subversive activities guided against its interest in Tibet. Nepali media has revealed Chinese intervention distinctively near the check points at the Indo-Nepal border to intercept Tibetan movement as well as to safeguard the Chinese interest that might be under threat from India's activity in Nepal. The Chinese were suspicious of Indian surveillance at the Sino-Nepal border in the sixties and later, when India and the West were more assertive. The case looks similar in the wake of the US aggressive commitment to make Nepal an active member of the "Indo-Pacific Strategy". From the passive poster of the past, China is becoming more assertive in Nepal and else at the moment.

---

10. U.S Department of State 2018 Report on International Religious Freedom: Nepal, https://www.state.gov/reports/2018-report-on-international-religious-freedom/nepal/ (Accecced on July 4, 2019)
11. Aditya Nath Speech in World Hindu Conference, Kathmandu https://www.youtube.com/watch?v=6G8YJ1Z4ydY

Likewise, after the Universal Peace Federation's Asia-Pacific Summit meeting sponsored by the Nepal Communist Party led PM, K. P. Sharma Oli's Government confirmed its sympathy to Christianity conversion against the constitutional provision. This sympathy was proven real when long time Christian associate C. K. Raut was surprisingly came into the mainstream who had no political mileage at all. The most scholars predicted it was under the grand designed strategy to give a pause to the conversion campaign in South Asia including China.

In such milieu, Nepal's fragility has multiple dimensions. Whether it will be a failed state or not is another question—but it is definite that its fragility will sensitize its burgeoning neighbours like India and China. The reasons for its fragility need special research in social science to find out the cause and effect in the global strategic stability in general and regional power balance in particular.

Chapter Two

Geopolitics - Mired At Foreign Interests

As we all know geography is the study of the land, living things in it, the climate, the people and their behaviour; as well as the overall environment on a given territory in a specific space. When we say study—it is a scientific analysis to gather knowledge. Interestingly, politics is the study of the society where human development takes place. Politics encompasses people - their socio-economic conditions, their relations - wants and values, power dynamics within and outside of the community. Similarly, polity is the power entity related with the governance. It is to improve status of the community it represents. Policy is the guideline that directs the course or the principal for action proposed by the governing body of the community vis-à-vis organization. In one way or other, they are related to ensure human development and their quality of life on a given territory.

For a student of social sciences with politics as the domain, it will be imperative to know the inter-dependency of geography with the politics and vice versa. In international relations, it is a matter of grave concern to understand their relationship which drives our research questions to formulate a viable theory. Harvey Starr opines that geography inextricably intertwines with the study of international relations as well as with the scholars who want to expertise in it.[12] International relations are dictated by geopolitics. And when we talk about the politics alone - it deals with the technique to governing the society. While geography is the study of the earth, its features and lives into it; politics remains very complicated phenomena due to its complexities on our relations. Nonetheless, it remains overriding to settle our disputes. And, by geopolitics, it is a relative analysis of influencing forces/powers in society and geographical relevancy to it that can accelerate its potentiality to others.[13]

12. Starr Harvey, 'On Geopolitcs', Routledge, 2013. p-2
13. Bhattarai, Umesh K. New Media and Its Role in Stabilizing Nepal: A Geopolitical Context. A chapter in an edited book "Media Diplomacy and its evolving role in the current geopolitical climate"

Shafick Osman[14] defined geopolitics in a talk program at the Institute for Defense Studies and Analyses (IDSA), New Delhi, India as it is not only a science, but it is a discipline that analyses various forces on a given territory in a specific space. As science deals with knowledge and to understand geopolitics - knowledge is not only sufficient. Of course, geopolitics is a branch of knowledge that needs expertise to be able to utilise the best of its advantage. If geopolitics is a discipline, we need to have a training that makes us willing to follow certain rules or to bear punishment if we break the rule. In other words, it is also an ability to control ourselves even at the time of crisis. Such professional ethics on geopolitics makes politicians, academia, and journalists successful to manage international relations on own favour.

Geopolitics—is it a challenge or an opportunity?

Nepal's geopolitics is debatable as a challenge as well as an opportunity from the days of its inception. Prithvi Narayan's *Dibya Upadesh* is the first of its kind that defines Nepal's strategy of national security vis-à-vis foreign policy. Later, King Mahendra adopted a non-alignment movement in the sixties which was guided by his philosophy. In pursuit to this movement, his son King Birendra proposed Nepal be declared as a "zone of peace" in 1975 during his coronation ceremony and was his earnest desire to institutionalize peace at one side which was also inspired by his ancestors' wish to maintain Nepal's neutrality and independence. Ironically, this proposal failed due to resistance from India. In fact, the non-alignment movement was also dormant at that stage after the disintegration of the Soviet Union and the end of the cold war. Emergence of China as a global power has again surfaced the possibility of a bipolarity once again. Russian Federation and China are together in many international issues.

India is also rising as a global power in Asia. USA and the West seldom use proxies to weaken China. But at the point, the US and European countries are also divided about looking at the Chinese pace of development and uses its capacity to their advantage. Among the European countries, mostly the Eastern who are less developed seek Chinese investment. Countries that were previously a part of the Warsaw Pact still pursue the Belt and Road Initiative (BRI) and Shanghai Cooperation Organization (SCO) for economic and military cooperation. In the Pacific region and in South Asia, the US interest confronts with the European Union in the economic and military cooperation

14. A Mauritius based professor specialized on geopolitics of Indian Ocean.

but coincides with the social interest in spreading of Christianity. In this point, India and China have common interest to repulse the Christian threat. But Nepal and its fragile politics has become a fertile platform for Christianity to spread which can socially be a potential threat to both the Asian giants, China and India. If Nepal fails to use its geopolitics tactfully, it will not only spoil itself but the spillover effect will challenge the stability of its neighbours as well.

Geopolitical Rivalries

China is aggressively committed to its BRI to connect to the rest of the world. The pace of development is very high in terms of infrastructure as well as in other service businesses. The financial aids to poor economies in terms of grant and loan has attracted most of the developing countries in Asia, Africa, Latin America and Europe. But at the same time, it has started a fresh debate as China is trying to lure up to trap the poor economies under its debt and use their facilities for its strategic gain. The negative reports of the BRI have confused even its neighbours who have already signed the project. Nepal is one of them.

India is not convinced with the BRI and motives behind the Chinese intensions. They have long-term dispute over border demarcation and have fought a major war in 1962. The recent Doklam incident is fresh. Although they have strong trade relations with each other and expect to increase more in the days to come but the strategic rivalry continues to show their influence in the sub-continent. Despite of their trade interest, India does not want China's strategic involvement in South Asia. The role it has played in Pakistan, Sri Lanka and in Maldives are few examples that India dislikes. India perceives entire South Asia as its homeland and wants under its sphere of influence. It considers the Chinese involvement as a challenge to its pivotal existence.

In fact, PM Narendra Modi's "neighbours first" policy has already failed to play a parental role. None of its neighbours are satisfied with the role it has played. The Gujaral Doctrine of reciprocity adopted in 1997 was not owned by its leaders and the bureaucracy rejected liberal policy towards its neighbours. This doctrine speaks as Indian contribution to its neighbours should be more than what it generates from them. Geographically, India is connected with all of its neighbours except Afghanistan, whereas none others are connected to any of them. So, India is the centre of gravity as far as trade is concerned. Transport link to all its neighbours passes through it. In fact, the use of natural resources of the entire South Asia is controlled by it as the entire trade is under its grip.

But, when there is the will there is the way, few other options are available even to its neighbours to trade outside South Asia. Pakistan, Sri Lanka, Bangladesh and Maldives have maritime access to connect to rest of the world, but countries like Nepal, Bhutan and Afghanistan are landlocked. When we talk about Nepal and Bhutan, they are not only India-locked from three sides but access to the North is also restricted, due to the high Himalayas as a natural barrier. Geography favours both of them to trade with India compared to the Tibetan region of China. Tibet is connected with Beijing through long distance railway link. Linking Tibet from the capital of both the countries across the Himalayas is costly. Plan to link Kathmandu by rail is undergoing for its feasibility, viability and environmental impact. As it is under the BRI project, the modality of the investment is crucial for both Nepal and China. Nepal prefers the project to be implemented under the Chinese grant. The total estimated cost as of today is not less than 3 Billion USD as revealed by the Nepal Transport Minister in the Kathmandu Investment Forum held in April 2019. The cost will definitely go high as the duration extends.

India has also committed for construction of railway link from Raxaul to Kathmandu. The agreement for this project has already been signed at the government level. India has agreed to construct it under the grant project. Nepal wants this railway to be of standard gauge so that the Chinese railway engine and locomotives can also be operated in the same track. The Indian railway track is based on broad gauge which is not compatible with standard gauge. How Nepali authority will manage this, time will tell.

Indian Connectivity Framework

India has been due to its central location at the crossroads of Asia is crucial for intruders. Maritime and continental realm of Asia passes through India. That is why Europeans and Central Asian nations have the passion to make their presence for trade and commerce here. The lucrative Indian Ocean is in priority for the USA, the EU, the African nations and even China in the quest for potential powers. The booming trade and economic development of India is continuously increasing day by day. Its trade and economic partnership, with both, the USA and China is guided by mutual cooperation although their strategic rivalry persists in many issues. Today, India is extensively engaged across the entire Asia-Pacific and beyond from Russia to Japan, China to Australia and at Africa and the Middle-east. It is a member of BRICS and SCO.

Under the "neighbourhood first" policy, India is continuously supporting Bangladesh, Sri Lanka, Nepal and the Maldives. Bhutan is supported under its different provision. Pakistan is due to its continued challenges posed in their bilateral relations disrupting India's connectivity efforts with its historical hinterland in the West and Central Asia has been a problem since 1947.

India's connectivity framework is principally designed to promote economic cooperation, cultural ties and develop strategic relationship with the countries in the Asia-Pacific region through continued engagement at the bilateral, regional and multilateral levels, thereby providing enhanced connectivity.[15] Under the greater interest, it has strategic vision to include maximum countries of South East Asia including South Asia in the Bay of Bengal Initiative for Multi-Sectoral and Economic Cooperation (BIMSTEC). It is an international organization encompassing 1.5 billion people, which have combined domestic product of 3.5 trillion USD. A total of 14 priority sectors have been identified with free trade agreement which is under negotiation.

BIMSTEC is highly prioritized by the Modi Government when he assumed his first tenure in 2014. The BRICS-BIMSTEC Outreach Summit was held in Goa in 2016 with renewed effort and strong commitment by India. On contrary to the South Asian Association for Regional Cooperation (SAARC), BIMSTEC is taken as a brainchild of India for regional connectivity and development. In this cooperation, Pakistan is intentionally excluded. SAARC is handicapped due to its own statute provision as it cannot continue its summit meeting if one of its members are unable to attend. Due to the Uri incident in Kashmir, India declined its participation in its Summit in 2016 held in Islamabad, where Nepal had to handover chairmanship to Pakistan. India blames Pakistan for sponsoring terrorism in its territory. Due to Indo-Pakistan strained bilateral relations, the future of SAARC as an institution is uncertain. India wants to substitute it with BIMSTEC and other connectivity efforts.

India has endorsed regional blocs connectivity efforts as Bangladesh, Bhutan, India and Nepal (BBIN) under which it has already signed its Motor Vehicle Agreements on June 15, 2015. As what Dr. Nilanjan Ghosh, Director of the Observer Research Foundation, Kolkata mentions about Bangladesh, China, India, and Myanmar (BCIM) regional bloc that India is likely to move forward

15. Delhi Policy Group's report on 'India and Connectivity Frameworks, November, 2017, p- 11-- https://www.delhipolicygroup.org/uploads_dpg/publication_file/india-and-connectivity-frameworks-1074.pdf

apparently in two folds as economic and strategically political. At the corner, there are cultural aspects that automatically come across. India's "Act East Policy" that PM Modi redefined its old "Look East Policy" of 1992 to reckon that opens trading corridors with its Eastern and South Eastern neighbours. It will be an endeavour to establish connectivity to unlock its tremendous untapped trading potential with its immediate South Asian neighbouring economies.[16]

As we know BCIM is still to be realized as a multi-model corridor and the first expressway between India and China to pass through Myanmar and Bangladesh, it will be game changer in Asia. Whether it is BCIM under the Indian initiative or the BRI of China, as long as they are contributing to the connectivity and development without any evil motives should not be objectionable to us. India is changing so as China and making connectivity and development efforts. PM Narendra Modi from the time of his first tenure—continued the connectivity project from "Look East Policy" to "Act East Policy".

India had launched the Look East Policy in 1992 with its strong willingness to open up to the world particularly the ASEAN nations as what Delhi Policy Group reports in 2017 under its India and Connectivity Frameworks. "India's Vision for Connectivity: A Discourse Analysis" by Antara Ghosal Singh revealed that PM Modi upgraded the old policy to a stronger "Act East Policy". India is said to believe that any global connectivity initiative must base on universally recognized international norms, good governance, rule of law, openness, transparency and equality which is what Official Spokesperson of MEA responded to a query on the participation of India in the OBOR and BRI Forum on May 13, 2017.[17] Simultaneously, PM Modi had also introduced "Neighbourhood First Policy" including Nepal on its priority but suspended most of the programmes due to various reasons. His Nepal policy was set back when Nepali leaders could not read accurately his mind as what he wanted in Nepal. In gist, his Nepal policy was flopped due to the international meddling into domestic affairs at the time of constitutional promulgation.

Although PM K. P. Sharma Oli has endorsed SAARC as an important tool to connect entire South Asian countries for cooperation, India is unlikely

---

16. Nilanjan Ghosh, The New Pathway: Is Sub- Regional BBIN a Role Model for Asian Connectivity, https://www.researchgate.net/publication/296969917_The_New_Pathway_Is_Sub-Regional_BBIN_a_Role_Model_for_Asian_Connectivity
17. https://www.mea.gov.in/media-briefings.htm?dtl/28463/Official_Spokespersons_response_to_a_query_on_participation_of_India_in_OBO

to promote it due to Pakistan's involvement in terrorist activities into it. PM Modi is keenly concerned to promote BIMSTEC that excludes Pakistan. In the changed scenario, Nepal Government under PM Oli had failed to understand the importance of solidarity of BIMSTEC members launching a military exercise after its 2018 Summit in Kathmandu. In a first such initiative, Nepal did not take part in a week long anti-terror exercise. It has been considered as a grave mistake of the Oli led Government to promote regional connectivity initiative sponsored by India.

BBIN council of ministers has approved it as sub-regional body in 1996. This interdependence and an economic effort were later formalized after a year in the Male Summit to agree upon connectivity and cooperation. It is an endeavour to focus to sub-continent's North East development for an intra-regional trade and investment, tourism, communication and energy resources.

Likewise—Bangladesh, China, India and Myanmar Economic Corridor (BCIM-EC) is an initiative to conceptualize potentiality for gains from the sub-regional economic cooperation within the member countries and beyond. If it is realised accordingly as multi-model corridor—definitely will be the first expressway between India and China passing through Myanmar and Bangladesh. Most scholars expect that all stakeholders of this initiative will have greater market for goods and services, energy with non-tariffs barriers, investment and infrastructure development, distribution of water and other natural resources.

In a nutshell, it will provide a comparative advantage to all by connecting people to people as a whole. In fact, it is expected to cover 1.65 million square kilometres encompassing more than 440 million people of the Yunnan province of China, Bangladesh, Myanmar and North East region of India. In addition, if it is connected with the BBIN, it will definitely have further comparative advantage to capture the entire South Asia Subcontinent in lieu of OBOR and BRI project that India is declining to accept because of Pakistan's involvement in China Pakistan Economic Corridor (CPEC) that it considers violating its right over the disputed region of Kashmir.

Territorial Encroachment and Nepal's Fate

India and China have both encroached Nepal's territory from its history. There are almost in 98 places, India has encroached border mainly in Susta, Kalapani,

Pasupatinagar, Bardia and Kanchanpur.[18] Lipiadhura and Lipulek are the most disputed areas where Nepal's land is encroached by both the countries. China and India both decided to use this place for their multi-model transit hub during PM Modi's first visit from May 14 to15 in 2015. This was a grave negligence from the world class leaders to use the territorial land of a small neighbour without formal consultation of its government.

The recent report published in *Business Standard* on May 31, 2019 claimed that China has encroached Nepal's land recently.[19] This was due to ongoing road expansion project in Tibet as per the Ministry of Agriculture. A total of 36 hectors of land in four districts adjoining the Chinese border now fall into the Chinese side due to this encroachment. China changed the direction of the river which now has been diverted to the Nepali side. In this way, Nepal would lose a hundred acres of land to the Tibetan side as quoted by the ministry in its report.

As per the survey of the ministry, six hectors of land in Humla's Bhagdare River and four acres of land in Karnali River area have been encroached and now falls in the Furang area of Tibet. Likewise, in Rasuwa district's Sanjen River, Bhurjung River and Jambukhola area - a total of six hectors of land has fallen into Tibet's Kerung area. As per the study, there are many other areas where encroachment is suspected that need to focus for survey as reported by the ministry.

Being a buffer in between two giants of Asia and keeping intact the territorial integrity is a big challenge for a small geopolitically deprived country like Nepal. In the north, there is the huge Himalayas as a natural barrier to connectivity and in the South, friendly but greedy to natural resources and selfish enough to look upon its own interest all the time. In such milieu, it had maintained its sovereignty and independence, when India was divided into small principalities and British East India Company consolidating power into it. China was under imperialist monarchy having Tibet as its protectorate state since 1720. It was the period in 1816 when British could control Nepal under its influence through the Sughauli Treaty after defeating a war of 1814-16.

The British philosophy was guided to keep Nepal under de-facto control through autocratic ruler. After 1947 when India was independent, Nehru

18. Responses to Indo-Nepal Relations: Journal 19 of Foreign Policy Research Centre, India - https://www.fprc.in/Pragya-NEPAL-19.pdf
19. https://www.business-standard.com/article/news-ani/china-encroaching-nepal-s-land-shows-government-survey-119053101022_1.html

followed a doctrine as continuation of the British philosophy. The Indian regime supported the democratic alliance under the Nepali Congress to abolish Rana autocracy at one side and in a chronicling deal forced Rana ruler to sign the Peace and Friendship Treaty in 1950. Most Nepali think they are deprived of their rights due to this unequal treaty—it is said unequal because there cannot be an equality which is not only landlocked—it is India locked by three sides. Besides to this, there is no comparison on power balance. The privilege and facilities provided by International Conventions are also deprived at times due to this treaty.

In the recent days, Nepal is warmed up with the new tussle in border dispute with its neighbours, India and China. In the wake of pending Eminent Persons' Group report on joint Indo-Nepal commitment to revise the Friendship Treaty of 1950, the publication of the new map showing the locations of Kashmir and Ladakh province with Nepal's adjoining territory by Indian establishment has revoked fresh confrontration between the two countries. According to various studies, more than 60,000 hectors of the Nepali territory have been encroached by its neighbours. Almost 374 square kilometres of Nepali land is under Indian control in Kalapani alone. Limpiadhura, Lipulekh and Kalapani are the areas encroached upon by both the neighbours. In May, 2015, India and China decided to use Lipulekh sector for multi-model transit hub to support their burgeoning trade. In fact, this was a grave mistake committed by both India and China to use the land of Nepal without a formal consultation with the Nepali government.[20]

Nepal is facing difficulty to safeguard its territorial integrity at the moment. The encroachment has started rapidly after the 1962's Indo-China War, when the withdrawing Indian Army occupied Kalapani as a likely route of ingress of the PLA forces into India. Indian Army took it under its control.

Realising the strategic importance of the territory, it continued strengthening its positions in the later dates. Some intellectuals in Nepal argued that the rulers at that time allowed the occupation by the Indian Army to safeguard their power but there is no concrete evidence to back this claim.

The authorised evidence of Nepal's ownership of this territory is the official map published by the British East-India Company after the 1816 Sugauli Treaty, which was the culminating point of the 1814-16 Anglo-Nepal War. This war had

20. https://myrepublica.nagariknetwork.com/news/safeguarding-our-territory/?categoryId=opinion&fbclid=IwAR1Jh9yEbEiWIFM8pdvNjCs3O33Rjtz04MPN7QTclfk5IAtK0Z0y4f1fmMU

ended with Nepal's defeat and losses of huge territory that it had brought under its rule after the unification by King Prithvi Narayan Shah and his successors in the later dates.[21]

Other than brief Nepal-Tibet War in 1856, Nepal had no major engagement after that in territorial war with its neighbours. Jung Bahadur Rana brought back Banke, Bardia, Kailali and Kanchanpur from the British as a reward of Nepal's support against Sepoy Mutiny in 1857. Thus, the final and sole evidence of Nepal's ownership over Kalapani is the map that had been finalised after the Sugauli Treaty.

The controversy that India has raised over the source of the Mahakali River, which is the international boundary, is the matter of dispute. Nepal claims that Limpiadhura is the source of the Mahakali River but India claims that a small tributary river named Kali is the actual boundary. Lipulekh and Kalapani are in the east of Limpiadhura, so Nepal says that entire area east of it belongs to Nepal.

Indian Prime Minister Narendra Modi had agreed, during his first visit to Nepal in 2014, that the territorial disputes between the two countries would be resolved bilaterally. Secretarial level joint committee had also been formed for that purpose. The sudden unilateral action from India has riled up Nepalis precisely for this reason.

The solution of this dispute that has surfaced must be resolved peacefully. For that, Nepal and India must sit down together. If necessary, we can also request Britain for mediation if India does not agree that Limpiadhura is the source of the Mahakali River. As the last resort, Nepal may also need to publish its own political map and proclaim its right over the territory in the International Court of Justice.[22]

This is happening at the time of great geopolitical struggle in Asia. Although the Himalayas is the natural barrier to connectivity, China has defied this barrier and is expanding connectivity. And, it is increasing its influence across the world in recent times. On the other hand, India is bent on securing its interests in its dealings with Nepal. In this situation, Nepal needs to demonstrate proactive diplomacy.

Nepal, in the past, played the "China card" against India and the "India card" against China. Resorting to this tactic would be counterproductive for Nepal.

21. Ibid.
22. Ibid.

India and China are no longer the rivals they used to be. President Xi Jinping has emphasized on strategic stability through strategic interaction within the framework of comprehensive partnership in our neighbourhood. Within this framework, we need to enhance our diplomatic skills not only to keep our territory intact, but also, to safeguard our interests. For this, first of all we must improve the deliverables of our domestic policy and governance.

Similarly, Nepal has failed to show its presence all along the borders to safeguard its territory. When the state fails to make its presence, it is likely to lose legitimacy. Nepal should seek peaceful solution bilaterally. It would be wise to properly regulate the borders so that, unwanted elements cannot take advantage of them illegally.[23]

In fact, in the words of the philosopher Thucydides, "... strong do what they have to do and the weak accept what they have to accept," Nepal need to be wise in tackling both the neighbours, carefully. In the latest President Xi Jinping's visit to PM Modi in South India, they agreed to a developmental model of 2+1 which PM Oli contradicted in his interview to *Kantipur Daily* on October 19, 2019 as Nepal wants to be a full-fledged trilateral strategic partner not as an extra either.

Fresh Solution for Kalapani Dispute

The Nepalis were very happy when all the meeting political parties agreed to raise the border dispute issue of the Limpiyadhura, Lipulekh and Kalapani against the Indian establishment. Most intellectuals also advised the Government of Nepal (GON) to solve the dispute through negotiations for safeguarding its territory. But we all know; it is not an easy task. Not realizing the gravity, it has asked the Secretary of the Ministry of Foreign Affairs to deal with the issue which has not been solved since 1962.

This issue was raised during the first visit of Indian Prime Minister Narendra Modi in 2014 and it had been decided that it would be resolved through the secretaries of the respective countries. But the problems continued. So, the Nepalis are not convinced with the GON's stand to solve the problems at the secretaries' level. The public demonstrations at the capital and other places continued, hence the GON is working in the line to send Madhav Kumar, the

23. Loc. Cit https://myrepublica.nagariknetwork.com/news/safeguarding-our-territory/?categoryId=opinion&fbclid=IwAR1Jh9yEbEiWIFM8pdvNjCs3O33Rjtz04MPN7QTclfk5IAtK0Z0y4f1fmMU

former Prime Minister of Nepal as its envoy to talk to PM Narendra Modi to solve the dispute as of December 5, 2019.

On Kalapani, some intellectuals have suggested to knock the door of the International Court of Justice (ICJ) because the Sughauli Treaty of 1816 has clearly mentioned Mahakali River as its western boundary originating from Limpiyadhura. Basically, the ICJ has two roles to ensure the international justice. Firstly, resolve legal disputes between the states and secondly, to advice the United Nations and its legislative bodies related to similar issues. But practically, it will not be so easy to ensure the rights of small countries. Mostly such disputes are petitioned by the right-based small countries against the interest-based strong one. As the working group report of the Law School of Chicago University in 2004 indicated that judges often apply law impartially and tend to favour the interest of their home country. Besides, the ICJ itself is becoming a victim of the conflicting interest of the states, who can manipulate its decision. Because of this reason, it has been widely criticized for its failure to become neutral.[24]

On the other hand, there are many instances where the border disputes have been settled through bilateral negotiations. As both India and Nepal have strong governments at the moment, if they wish earnestly, they can resolve the Kalapani issue without delay. The solution could be on the line of India and Bangladesh that solved their enclaves' adjustment in June 2015, which was pending pursuant to the Land Budgetary Agreement 1974. The way PM Narendra Modi demonstrated his skill in resolving such isuues, he can also show the similar attitude to manage dispute with Nepal provided it produces enough evidences of its right.[25]

If India considers the Kalapani area as of its prime strategic interest, one possible option can be to exchange land between the two countries. For this, India should provide Nepal an access to the Bay of Bengal.[26] As there is massive public resentment towards the Indian policy over Nepal, majority of the people might strongly oppose this proposal. It is the responsibility of the government to convince the people if it is a positive one.

The biggest drawback to resolving this issue bilaterally is the mistrust among the parties. The internal politics is badly ruined by selfish desires. The national

24. https://myrepublica.nagariknetwork.com/news/reclaiming-our-land/?categoryId=81&fbclid=IwAR0g1KFRZO701IuR4I1u3Qple9qcsOTIFlHZ0bIoQJNH7ozoL5fzlvrCgkw
25. Ibid.
26. Ibid.

interest is compromised for parties and even individual interest. If such trend continues, the border encroachment can never be stopped. It is high time for the Nepalis to show their solidarity to pressurize political leaders and improve the quality of decision-making in favour of national interest.

Xi Jingpin's Nepal Visit and its Impact

President Xi Jinping paid a very short state visit to Nepal on October 12, 2019 after 23 years of his predecessors with a long-lasting message of China's firm commitment to turn "land-locked" Nepal into a "land-linked" by boosting connectivity between the two countries. Altogether 20 pacts were signed including 18 memorandum of understanding and two letters of intent with USD 500 million in economic aid.

The major hallmark in their relations had started with a joint ideological opening between the Communist Party of Nepal and the Chinese Communist Party through a two-day conference for cementing their bonds just three weeks before the visit of President Xi to Nepal. It has been considered that the conference paved a significant ideological convergence between Beijing and Kathmandu. The intelligentsia having a strong belief as the Chinese Communist Party had played a crucial role to unite the former Maoist and the United Marxist Leninist into one before the parliamentarian election has now been proved logically after this conversion conference.

In fact, this entire mess was developed with the hegemonic influence of India that it had vehemently shown during the economic embargo after Nepal's promulgation of a new constitution in 2015. Development and diversity on trade and transit were basic demands of the people after Nepal entered to a republican model. Anger against the Indian establishment favored K. P. Sharma Oli's stand to open the Northern front for trade and transit in the quest of diversity. People supported his election agenda and now, he looks firm to implement them.

Among all the pacts, there are two which seem contentious having long-term implications in Nepal's interest. Firstly, the Mutual Legal Assistance Treaty (MLAT) can be taken as extradition agreement in other language; which China can use to punish against the Tibetan refugees exiled in Nepal. Although the Ministry of Law, Justice and Parliamentary Affairs said that there is no provision for executing judgment in this treaty but, no one can belief that the powerful China will not defame Nepal falling to fulfill its commitment to human rights considering its size and the geopolitical constraints. There are ample of examples of deportation pressure to Tibetan refugees by the Chinese establishment in the past.

From the very beginning of the China-Nepal relations, it is reiterating commitment to "One-China Policy" though there are more than 20,000 Tibetan refugees sheltering in Nepal. Due to international pressure, Nepal can neither deport them nor speak against the Chinese atrocities in Tibet. Consequently, it is used as a transit hub for Tibetans in their plight to India and the West. Before departing from Kathmandu, President Xi pointedly used the Nepali soil to send an unambiguous message that "anyone attempting to split China in any part of the country will end in crushed bodies and shattered bones".[27] Considering his nature and humbleness, this is a very strong message, whomever he passed to.

Coming to joint communiqué, China-Nepal agreed to become "strategic partner" for development. This statement has kept other partners suspicious about Nepal's motive. Harsh V. Pant writes about this as Modi government has made an outreach to Nepal a priority in the "Neighbourhood First policy". Yet, the growing presence of the Chinese in Nepal is a reality that India can do little about. He insists that India should be providing an alternative narrative for a fresh India-Nepal ties. He looks rationale by thinking about how India-Nepal relations can be strengthened as prior to the embargo in 2015. PM Oli has also mentioned in his interview that Nepal can make India too a "strategic partner" just as China is. He categorically mentioned being a partner strategically does not mean we are militarily aligned—yes, he is correct. But it is definitely against the spirit of the nonalignment and neutrality. Does this mean Nepal is deviating from its age-old foreign policy dogma?

Nepal's foreign policy is guided by non-alignment, neutrality, principles of Panchsheel and the UN Charter. Nepal's development partners are supportive as Nepal has shown strong commitment to international peace and harmony. So, before signing the Joint Communiqué with China as a "strategic partner," Nepal should have deliberately thought about our its position in non-alignment and neutrality as well.

The current Nepal's Foreign Minister Pradeep Gyawali interpreting of the China-Nepal's "strategic partnership" as a "new terminology of friendship" has

27. Harsh V. Pant, Xi goes to Nepal, Observer Research Foundation (ORF) article published online on October 17, 2019. https://www-orfonline-org.cdn.ampproject.org/c/s/www.orfonline.org/research/xi-goes-nepal-56744/?amp

confused most intellectuals. Strategic partnership is not really a military alliance as it had been thought in the periods of Cold War. Prof. Dhurba Kumar rightly mentioned in his article in *Kantipur Daily* on October 25, 2019 that the military alliance is really formed to counter the common enemy nation whereas strategic partnership is specifically for the development in the China-Nepal case. But, if we see the nature of few other pacts among the 20, the suspicion goes further. So, it will be wise on the part of the Government of Nepal to clear it to the people as early as possible otherwise, the confusion will degrade the government itself. Basically, the confusion has been created because of the minister's lack of knowledge and ability to interpret the subject matter and the media overreacted into the issues.

Xi's Interest in Nepal's Stability

A reliable source in Kathmandu revealed immediately after President Xi Jinping visit as he categorically inquired on how Nepal's political stability can be restored? He was eager to know the modalities of the 12 Point Agreement and provisions for secularism, republic and federalism. He was cautious on the monarchical role in the present context. In a series of meetings with the mainstream political party leaders his concern was related to how Nepal became secular instead of a majority Hindu population and why federalism is not functioning effectively after four years of its existence.

As China being a very close neighbour and prominent partner in development - the questions are not only genuine but also, carry important value for the entire Nepalis. Neither the secularism nor the federalism had been directly chosen by the Nepali mass. The survey reports by few parliamentarians were also not clearly transparent for the public. Even the monarchy was hastily ousted in Nepal, so it has been a burning question for all of us including President Xi as the source indicates.

It is open to all that federalism is very costly for poor country like Nepal. In fact, most people demanded for decentralization not federalism. It was imposed by the West and specially the European Union as most intellectuals suspect. To maintain numerous governments, the heavy taxation has become the burden for most of us. The rising inflation has increased the cost of living for the poor and the middle-class people.

The trade deficit with neighbours due to import based market has become major problem to balance domestic economy. The industrial base is weak and unemployment is alarming. To engage youths, government has encouraged foreign employment, notwithstanding the long-term impact of it—Nepal is becoming fragile day by day. In such scenario, if President Xi Jinping has raised concerns about our situations it means that he is quite conversant and serious about the stability of Nepal.

Chapter Three

Stability—A Thrive to Development

Nepal's stability was characterized by its geopolitics. In the ancient and medieval period when connectivity was really poor—the tiny and small principalities had no reach to rest of the world. The imperial powers like British East India Company and the former Soviet Union created fear among the sensitive leaders in this part of the Himalayas. Chinese monarchy had poor control over Tibet from Beijing till Communist Party of China under Mao Tse Tung invaded it in 1950. The real time strategist King Prithvi Narayan Shah foresaw the future of divided principalities to counter the offensive if the aforementioned forces would have invaded across the Himalayas from the north or, via Chure and Mahabharat range from the south. To repulse the offensive, he decided to unite Nepal for its survival and stability in the future.

Prithvi Narayan's Legacy

King Prithvi Narayan Shah had a clear philosophy on state affairs as he revealed in his *Dibya-Upadesh* (Divine Counsel) to his countrymen. His understanding of Nepal's "geopolitics" was not only clear but also proved to be a long-term prescription to handle its huge neighbours after his death. He was one of the pioneers among the strategists of his time emphasizing on economic prosperity, states' monetary regulations and scientific agricultural farming. Besides these, his vision on the neighbouring powers was so sharp that enabled his successors to formulate military and foreign policies effectively, even after his death in 1775.

On contrary to his ideological supremacy, some historians blame him as pro-Hindu as he claimed Nepal as the *"real-hindustan"*.[28] Perhaps, he had opined it as India was previously ruled by the Moguls (Muslims) after the Mourya (Hindu) and then by the British who spread Christianity and forced Hindus to follow their religion. His "real-hindustan" statement has been wrongly interpreted by non-Hindus and criticised his overall unification campaign as his autocratic wish to rule Nepal. After 244 years of his death, Nepal is still fighting for and against a Hindu state. The Nepali Constitution of 2015 declared Nepal a "secular"

28. Rawal, Ram Bahadur. (2011, November 13). Rastrabad Vs Rastraghat. *Nepal Weekly*. 17-18.

that has dissatisfaction among the Hindus worldwide. As a consequence, PM Modi on his second innings as prime minister of India has signalled through the Chief Minister of Uttar Predesh, Aditya Nath Yogi that Nepal should be declared a Hindu state again. To counter this statement, the US has issued a report connecting religion into its foreign policy under "Report on International Freedom-2018" as India has been spending to save Hinduism in Nepal. This is likely to create further sensation as well.

In fact, King Prithvi Narayan's vision is still valid in the present Nepali context. The gist of his *Dibya-Upadesh* revealed that Nepal could not only be united from his individual effort but was possible through collective endeavour. So, he mentioned it as a garden with flowers of four tribes and thirty-six castes *(char barna and chhatish jaat)*. Although he mentioned categorically four tribes and thirty-six castes, but one should understand that he meant all natives are the same for the nation who were residing that time in Nepal.

To understand his states' economic policy, he seems to be protective of the native traders as he urged to discourage foreign traders beyond *Parsa-gadi*, near present Indo-Nepal border. If they were allowed to come inside, they would have captured the entire domestic trade, consequently, natives would have been deprived off. He insisted to ban foreign fabrics and garments so as to promote domestic cottage industry. He had a view that if foreign traders were allowed, the national monetary reserves would descend and country's economy fails. He emphasized to grow herbs and other agriculture products including natural resources to export and increase foreign reserves. In the social justice front, he insisted as justice and bribery are interlinked and the latter is the worst enemy of the state. According to him - who seeks bribe and who provides are both criminals by law.[29]

His *Divya Upadesh* is probably the single most significant document which explains the Gorkha conquest as contribution to his endeavour to unify Nepal. Bipin Adhakari highlights the amazed confidence of Nepal's unifier as he asserted his preparedness to withstand imminent Turk, Magar and Mughal threat.[30] On contrary to Adhikari's understanding of the threat as he envisaged, the East India Company had already entered India in 1608 and had expanded colliding other European establishments like Spain, Portugal, France and Netherlands, so he

29. Acharya, *Nepal ko Samchhipta Britant.*
30. Dr Bipin Adhikari, "The Divba Upadesh of Prithvi Narayan Shah," an article published in the Spotlight magazine.

missed out British as a major threat to Prithvi Narayan in his article. In addition, the British were found engaging in constant conflicts over trading monopoly in India, China and South East Asia.[31] The Mughals may be a threat at the early stage but the Magers, he mentioned was internal.

His foremost military tactics was based on "*Jai Katak Garnu-Jhiki Katak Na-garnu*" that means "if somebody attacks-attack him back, but never attack first". Prithvi Narayan's *Dibya Upadesh* was inspired by top world thinkers, warriors and the philosophers like Kautilya, Sun Tzu, Thucydides, Machiavelli, and Napoleon.

Box 1.1: Dibya Upadesh by King Prithvi Narayan Shah

- Nepal is a small yam between two stones, indicating Nepal's location between China and India.
- Both the people who take or give bribe are the enemies of nation. There would be no sin executing them.
- Nepal is a garden of four caste and thirty-six sub castes.
- Even if there is settlement in places with mines/quarries, relocate the settlement and operate mine.
- Maintain a treaty of friendship with China and also the emperor of South (company) - he knew if Hindustan is united, it will be difficult for him- so he will seek places for forts in the hills.
- Prepare forts without burdening the people.
- Set traps in the trials
- Do not go down to the plains to fight
- Withdraw to the hills to fight- chure pass can be much used.
- Store arms and ammunitions three to five to seven second lines.
- Ganga is also line of defense.
- Strength of Nepal lies in the forts
- In higher places- cannons should be deployed.
- In the gaps in the mountains-an iron door should be built.
- Behind the doors, on the higher place- cannon should be sited and guarded by troops. If so, there is no chance of being ambushed or spying.

Source: L.F. Stiller, S. J.32

31. "A Brief History of the British East India Company"---- http://learn.culturalindia.net/brief-history-british-east-india-company-essay.html
32. L.F. Stiller, S.J, Prithvi Narayan Shah in the Light of Dibya Upadesh, Catholic Press, Ranchi, India 1968 (p 38-57).

Prithvi Narayan's Dibya Upadesh Vs Other Philosophers

King Prithvi Narayan Shah is said to be inspired by Kautilya alias Chanakya alias Vishnugupta who was guru as well as politico-economic adviser of Chandragupta Maurya, his son Bindusara and grandson Emperor Ashoka. He is also known as Indian Machiavelli among the Western intellectuals but in the Indian civilization he is much ahead to establish the foundation of *Arthashastra* compared to other philosophers of the world.[33] Kautilya's *Arthashastra* is a unique inclusion of politics, statecraft, diplomacy, finance, social justice and law as well as battle craft, which are equally applicable even today.

In ancient India, the thinkers were divided in two schools of war - diplomacy and interstate relations. They were further subdivided into *Dharma-yuddha* (ethical warfare) and *Kuta-Yuddha* (devious warfare) schools. Both the schools were not exclusive and practitioners of each school were not informed by the principles and methods of the other. The best example of this is the great *Mahabharata* war in which one can see both the schools of thought in operation: in this war the victory went to the practitioners of the *kuta-yuddha* school although the war itself has always been described as *dharma-yuddha.* The great strategist lord Krishna, according to the Hindu mythology, did not touch weapons but used all diplomatic techniques in favour of the Pandavas. His own force was fighting against him and his allies. But his manoeuvre and tactics played a significant role to make the Pandavas, the winner against the Kauravas. In the other epic war, the *Ramayana*, although both the stream of thoughts was at work, the victory went to the *dharma-yuddha* (righteous/ethical) school.

To elaborate Kautilya's *Arthashastra*, scholars define *artha* as wealth or power and *dharma* as political virtue or ethical and moral issues in statecraft. On the basis of an in-depth study, it is realized that *dharma* regulates *artha* in the Indian tradition.[34] It has been realized over a period of time as the Indian traditional strategic thought were guided with the concept of *dharma* as a set of rules that bound the ruler as well as the ruled one to follow a set of discipline to govern statecraft. It helped to follow strong moral as well as ethical lifestyle in contrast to present system where everyone wants to break the existing power in their own favour. It is like confrontation between rising powers with the established powers in the contemporary world.

33. Luitel, Tilak Prasad. *Kautiliya Arthsastra*. 2016. Preface.
34. Gautam, Predeep Kumar. "Understanding Dharma and Artha in Statecraft through Kautilya's Arthashastra". IDSA p.7—8.

As per Kautilya, *artha* is wealth synonymously power, which is a means but not an end. It has to be protected by the state or the owner itself. In the materialistic world where all the business is related to profit and loss like the way merchants consider but the state has a superior role to protect all its citizens residing in the state. His *Matsyana* philosophy talks about the way big fish swallows small one—in the same way big investors or merchants exploit petty investors or businessmen to survive. He insisted that the king should adopt policies that would lead the state to prosperity and avoid those that lead to decline.[35]

Prithvi Narayan's *Dibya Upadesh* is heavily dominated by the *Matsayana* philosophy while he talks about fiscal policy of Nepal. Kautilya was with a view to arrange markets to sale domestic products through one door policy whereas distribution points for foreign products should be several. But in either case people must be protected by the state not to be cheated by merchandize either.[36] Kautilya had propounded his *Arthashastra* nearly around 350-275 BCE, which was lost near the end of the Gupta Empire until it was rediscovered in 1915.

Regarding the foreign policy, *Arthashastra* proclaims unfavourable results in bad policy. Although diplomacy is an art and has no direct connection with the ideals, but indirectly, it is guided through it. If the invading state is rising, then the weak state tries to avert invasion by offering gifts or making a treaty of peace. Similarly, if weak state is not of strategic importance or may be better to leave aloof or can pay better dividend in the future - the treaty may be fruitful for invading one. Perhaps, the East India Company was inspired to follow this policy as Tibet could be more lucrative to expand business in the Western Chinese market as a critical part of the imperial chessboard[37] and on the contrary, Nepal as merely a stepping stone.

The East India Company had a fear from the very beginning that if the Soviet Union would invade Tibet - it could have directly threatened its existence in India. Similarly, as Tibet was a protectorate state of China since 1720 - it was reluctant to have a direct confrontation with the Qing dynasty across the Himalayas considering the lengthy line of communication to maintain its army from India. Due to these reasons, the British were trying to have strong position

35. Ibid.
36. Loc.cit Luitel. P-112
37. Sanjaya Upadhya, *Nepal and the Geostrategic Rivalry between China and India.* Routledge, 2016. P-1

in Nepal trapping its autocratic rulers through the treaties as what Kautilya had envisaged. King Prithvi Narayan had already envisioned the British attitude in this part of the world.

Let us examine the Sun Tzu's principle with respect to King Prithvi Narayan's *Dibya Upadesh.* Sun Tzu was a Chinese general, who was credited to authoring *The Art of War*[38] published during the fifth Century BC, with a very popular quote such as:

> *... if you know the enemy and know yourself you need not to fear the results of a hundred battles*
>
> *- Sun Tzu*

Sun Tzu was also popular as Sunzi and has been suspected whether such a person actually existed or whether what has come down to us as Bingfa (BF) was a compilation of the sayings of several strategists. Bingfa is known as "the art of war" that teaches the military professions on how to seize the situation for the betterment of a state.[39] The person like Sun Bin later spread Sun Tzu's idea within China which had several states that time. King Pritvi Narayan's *Dibya Upadesh* has some flavour of Sun Tzu's Bingfa into it. Sun Tzu's philosophy on how to be a great leader and ensure on your endeavour in life is summed up as a leader leads by example, you have to believe on yourself, appear weak when you are strong - and strong when you are weak and so on.[40] For detail, refer Annex C attached.

Likewise, Thucydides - an Athenian historian, political philosopher and general recounted Peloponnesian War in the fifth century BC between Sparta and Athens. He is considered as a father of "scientific history" because of his strict standards of evidence-gathering and analysis of "cause and effect" without reference to intervention by the gods. A Harvard scholar - Alexander Kemos[41] wrote that Thucydides was the first to describe international relations as anarchic and immoral. His views on interstate politics lack regulation and justice. In the "Melian Dialogue"- he wrote about interstate relations as:

> *... the strong do what they have the power to do and the weak accept what they have to accept*
>
> *- Thucydides*

38. Sun Tzu- Art of War - http://classics.mit.edu/Tzu/artwar.html (accessed on March 4, 2018)
39. The details about Bingfa or art of war of that time has been mentioned in Appendix
40. Eric Jackson. Sun Tzu's 31 Best Pieces of Leadership Advice. https://www.forbes.com/sites/ericjackson/2014/05/23/sun-tzus-33-best-pieces-of-leadership-advice/#108403d35e5e
41. The Influence of Thucydides in the Modern World - http://www.hri.org/por/thucydides.html

For him, international relations allow the mighty to do as they wish and force the weak to suffer as they must. His philosophy is highly regarded as "Thucydides trap" when we talk about interstate relations in political science. King Prithvi Narayan's *Dibya Upadesh* is influenced by his opinion. He regarded the British Raj in India as expansionist, cunning and shrewd, and China as the sleeping giant - if awakened may keep the neighbours in trouble. So, he wanted a united Nepal to counterpoise both the powers. He understood the importance of geopolitics very well.

To define geopolitics, according to Shafick Osman,[42] it is not only science but it is a discipline that analyses various forces on a given territory in a specific space. Perhaps, he may be true as science deals with knowledge and to understand geopolitics - knowledge is not only sufficient. Of course, geopolitics is a branch of knowledge which one has to be expert upon to become master on it. If geopolitics is discipline, we need to have a training that makes us willing to follow certain rules otherwise to bear punishment if we break the rule. In other words, it is also an ability to control ourselves even at the time of crisis.[43]

King Prithvi Narayan had no formal training and education, but he was evolved with prevailing situation to understand contemporary politics. In his childhood, he had seen how his father Nara Bhupal Shah was defeated in Nuwakot. Being an enthusiastic prince, he was groomed to become a king in the small principality of Gorkha, who turned to be more ambitious later. It is said he was blessed with Guru Gorakhnath as wherever he touches there, he would be victorious. Although, it is superstition but evidence supports as blessing came true on the part of King Prithvi Narayan Shah. His daughter-in-law Rajendra Laxmi and his youngest son Bahadur Shah later expanded Nepal as per his wish despite of personal rivalry in several issues that brewed as a part of palace conspiracy.

Nepal after Prithvi Narayan

King Prithvi Narayan died at the age of 51 due to high fever. It is said he was attacked by a tiger while he was hunting it in Nuwakot, the place known as

42. A Mauritius based professor specialized on geopolitics of Indian Ocean revealed in a talk program at Institute for Defense Studies and Analyses, New Delhi, India.
43. Bhattarai, Umesh K. New Media and Its Role in Stabilizing Nepal: A Geopolitical Context. A chapter in an edited book "Media Diplomacy and its evolving role in the current geopolitical climate"

Devighat near Trisuli. Before his death, he could annex areas up to the Tista River including Sikkim in the east but his westbound expansion was left pending. His elder son King Pratap Singh Shah succeeded the throne in the mist of controversy as to who should be the successor either himself, or his younger brother Bahadur Shah. Pratap Singh was not competent and courageous like his father and believed to be enjoying luxurious life. On the contrary, Bahadur Shah was more influenced to his father's quality though he lacked formal education. He was groomed with military customs and was just 13-years-old when his father died.

King Pratap Singh Shah also died a natural death just after two years of his ascending the throne in 1777. As palace courtiers were already divided, it further brewed conspiracy as to who should be the regent of Rana Bahadur Shah, the infant son of King Pratap Singh Shah. The palace decided to go for a joint regency under Queen Rajendra Laxmi, mother of King Rana Bahadur Shah and uncle of Prince Bahadur Shah. There was personality clash between the brother and the sister-in-law in many issues but they remained committed to fulfill King Prithivi Narayan's desire to create an integrated Nepal.

Bahadur Shah took a lead to expand Nepal and later, Queen Rajendra Laxmi also supported the campaign. Although they were strong rival and imprisoned as well as sent on exile to each other whoever seized the power. Bahadur Shah spent most of his time to expand Nepal westward. He fought a battle with Tibet and China in 1788-92 that he lost. Although he could succeed integrating Nepal in the west as what King Prithvi Narayan wished for, he failed the battle with China that lead to his downfall in the history of Nepal.

In King Rana Bahdur's tenure, Bhimsen Thapa remained the centre of power as his core adviser till he was assassinated by his step-brother Sher Bahadur Shahi. After the Ranamukteshor incident, Bhimsen Thapa emerged to power as de-facto ruler under the regency of Queen Lalit Tripura Sundari as King Griban Yuddha was an infant. Bhimsen Thapa seized all the powers and declared himself as the first prime minister and the Commander-in-Chief of Nepal. He exercised his absolute autocratic rule for 31 years.

In the later dates, he resumed westward expansion of Nepal that King Bahadur Shah had left incomplete. Under his command, Nepal fought a battle with British India in 1814-16 that it lost and was compelled to sign the Sughauli Treaty, whichshaped the present Nepal. His role in Nepal's politics has remained controversial. His suicide in custody on the charge of state conspiracy is still a mystery. The way he rose to power and declined is quite obvious as most autocratic rulers face. The historians are still divided on his personality as to whether he was a patriot or a traitor.

The rise of Jung Bahadur as the prime minister and "Sri 3 Maharaj" was similar to Bhimsen Thapa. He assassinated 32 high-ranking courtiers including the prime minister overnight on a cover of the queen's order, who was holding the executive power of Nepal that time. She was on hike of anger to find out the murderer of General Gagan Singh Bhandari overnight from the emergency assembly she had called and tasked Jung Bahadur to give the instant result. This incident is widely known as *Kot Parba* in Nepal. He emerged to power through this incident. The historians claim that Jung Bahadur visited early morning, the next day to Lainchour, where the British residents used to live. From then onwards, he established the Rana family rule for 104 years. He pleased the British by all means. The royalties were virtually imprisoned by the Rana prime minister having full executive power of the country.

Rana Autocracy

Kot massacre was a blessing for Jung Bahadur Rana to come to power. By nature, he was shrewd and clever. He was impressed with the rising British power all over the world. It is said that the actual reason for him to visit Britain and France was to assess their power. He was convinced with the British influence in the region and abroad. That is why he was too inclined to the British thereby ignoring northern Tibet and the Chinese power. He supported each and every action of British outrightly. Showing British at the back, he established a new feudal model to transfer the executive prime-ministerial power to the next younger brother after the elder one.

Although Jung Bahadur was a close ally to the British, he was not in favour of allowing the Nepali youths to join the British Army. He resisted the recruitment process in 1858 imposing punishment defying states' order. He was vigilant and informed about the plight of the youths will make the nation weak. The British could not openly offend him and suspended the recruitment for some time but continued covertly.

It was Bir Shumser who allowed the British to recruit the Nepalis openly. Chandra Shumser also followed him to please them. He supported the British to crash the Tibetan rebellion of 1905 in the Yunnan province, which is widely known as the Boxer Rebellion.[44] The rebellion was guided against the Qing Dynasty by the Tibetan Lamas. The Qing Dynasty invited Christian missionaries to crash them. The Nepal Army took part in the support of the British per se the Qing Dynasty under Chandra Shumser's order.

Although there are no concrete historical evidences on Nepal's support to the Boxer Rebellion by Chandra Shumsher, there is enough ground to suspect him as he was successful to conclude the Nepal-Britain Treaty of 1923 that favoured Nepal in many ways. It rectified some of the controversial provisions of the Sugauli Treaty of 1816 that undermined Nepal's independence and sought referral of the arbitration of the East India Company as Nepal being a tributary state of the British Empire. There was also a provision to limit Nepal to carry on independent foreign policy as well.

Recognizing Nepal's limited sovereignty, Chandra Shumsher raised this issue to the visiting Prince of Wales later Edward VIII to Kathmandu in 1921 to have a new peace treaty to grant Nepal an independent sovereignty and freedom to formulate foreign policy at its own decision. Later. it was agreed as the first of such a treaty between Nepal and Britain that was recorded in the League of Nations. This treaty cleared Nepal's position as an independent sovereign nation in the international status. The sole credit for this goes to Chandra Shumsher and it was due to his support to the British in many ways including the Boxer Rebellion in Tibet.

The reason why Chandra Shumsher's request was honoured by the British was his wholehearted support to them and that could be Nepal's support for the success of the Boxer Rebellion. The emerging threat from the communist in Russia was envisaged strong enough for not only to the Qing Dynasty in China but also to Nepal as it was also under threat. The British would have quickly smelt the threat to them and perhaps, encouraged the imperial Qing Dynasty and Nepal to unite against the rising Bolsheviks Revolution in Russia.

The Ranas used their instinct to use British to prolong their regime. Jung Bahadur and Chandra Shumser visited Britain as the prime minister. They could assess the British power in-depth. Their cordial nexus with the British enabled

---

44. International Encyclopedia of Military History, page 576, https://books.google.com.np/books?id=ELDlCAAAQBAJ&pg=PT622& lpg=PT622&dq=Role+of+Nepal+in +Boxer +Rebellion+in+ Tibet&source=bl&ots=hYHOe5qV (assessed on May 18, 2018)

Nepal to remain independent and free even in the mist of colonial rule. Nepal remained stable under the Ranas but development and education was rampant. They were envisioned with the idea that if the Nepalis will be educated and Nepal is open to the rest of the world their regime will be challenged. British were quite familiar with their weaknesses and strength of the Nepali people - they used it for their advantage at the most.

Foundation for Popular Resentment

By the time India got independence from the British in 1947, the wave of democracy had already started chasing Nepal's politics. Notwithstanding the changing wave, the Ranas were just in a lasting sleep when the Nepali Congress established first political party in 1946. The monarchy was in virtual house arrest by the Rana rulers. The Rana intimidation and torture forced King Tribhuvan to establish nexus with the like-minded democrats including the Nepali Congress, which was already in existence in India.

Leaders like B. P. Koirala, M. P. Koirala, Tanka Prasad Acharya, and Puspa Lal Shrestha were in limelight that time. The Koirala brothers had a close nexus with established Indian leaders, who fought independence war along with them against the British. They created a platform with the Indian establishment to seek asylum for King Tribhuvan in India. In a very chronicling situation, the king drove his entire family excluding his grandson King Gyanendra to the Indian Embassy at Sital Niwas.

The two Koirala brothers, M. P. and B. P. were the rising stars of the Nepali politics in exile. They were educated equally in Indian schools. B. P. was bit smarter and more vocal compared to M. P. to respond the ideas and events.[45] They were groomed well as political activists and as student leaders in India when their family was in exile. The Gandian upsurge was in peak in the subcontinent that inspired them to involve in the freedom fight against the British rule in India. Both were tested by time but B. P. suffered much in detention and exile, as he was much vocal as well as rigid in his stand.

At times, both the brothers had bitter rivalry from philosophical perspective but overall were respectful to each other. By nature, M.P. was inaccessible to all and introvert compared to his younger brother. For those who knew him closely and even by adversaries agree that M. P. went against the political current and

45. Koirala MP, A Role in a Revolution, Jagadamba Prakashan, Nepal P-VIII

avoided taking populist positions. Perhaps, because of this reason, he ultimately became isolated in national politics.[46]

It had been most surprising as to how M. P. was picked up for prime minister in the interim constitution soon after the dissolution of the Rana-Congress coalition government in November 1951. The central leadership of the Nepali Congress was unanimously in favour of B. P. Koirala to lead the government but a personal letter from Indian Prime Minister Jawahar Lal Nehru to King Tribhuvan preferred M. P. as next prime minister of Nepal.[47]

B. P. revealed later as the Indian leaders with whom they worked together to fight against the colonial rule changed their attitude towards Nepal after achieving independence. Perhaps M. P. who was quite young and immature that time compared to Indian politicians was bullied whenever he tried to stand firmly for Nepal's favour. Ganesh Raj Sharma revealed in the preface of the book *A Role in a Revolution* by M. P. Koirala as a reason for his resignation from prime minister quoted by Rishikesh Shah who criticized India pursuing Nepal as follows:[48]

> *... The Government of Nepal will consult with the Government of India on such matters that will seek advice and opinion with a view to promoting better coordination from the latter on matters of establishing relations with any foreign country with a view to promoting better coordination in the policy of two countries ... especially on matters of Nepal's relationship with Tibet and China, special advice will be sought from the government of India.*

To ignore Indian request was tough for any prime minister so as to M. P. He consulted King Tribhuvan who was against the text as designed about Nepal's independence and sovereignty. This was taken as a grave dishonour to Nepal but neither king nor the prime minister took a right decision to address Indian proposal appropriately. M. P. would have continued as prime minister and dealt India diplomatically. But he opted resignation that tarnished his image at home and lost political goodwill with India for ever.

The similar case happened with B. P. dealing India when he became the prime minister. It was in 1959 when Indian PM Jawahar Lal Nehru addressed his parliament as the entire Northern Himalayas is its boundary and any aggression

46. Ibid.
47. Ibid.
48. Shah, Rishikesh, Modern Nepal (Manohar, 2001).

on Nepal will be considered as attack to India ignoring Nepal's independent and sovereign status. This statement was against an incident when a Nepali soldier was killed by the PLA in the Sino-Nepal border. PM B. P. Koirala rebutted Nehru as Nepal's frontier cannot be India's border and its security responsibility cannot be outsourced to any nation.[49]

Immediately after this incident B. P. Koirala renewed Peace and Friendship Treaty with the People's Republic of China in 1960, and side by side- King Mahendra played a crucial role to enhance connectivity through the Kodari Highway. Consequently, both the personalities were discredited in the eyes of the Indian leaders. The relation was further soured when King Birendra purchased anti-aircraft guns with China. This led India imposing an economic embargo to Nepal for more than a year.

Likewise, King Gyanendra proposed China as an observer in the South Asian Association for Regional Cooperation (SAARC) in 2005 that made India resent towards the royalty. Covertly, it supported the Maoist insurgency and in a very chronicling situation the Nepali Congress leader G. P. Koirala (M. P. and B. P.'s younger brother) formed a solidarity to go for the republic state in 2006. India was successful to play for Rana's out in 1950, it could change Panchayat regime and compel King Birendra to become constitutional monarchy in 1990; and at the last under a grand design to overthrow King Gyanendra and abolish royalty from Nepal.

Before reaching to this, it would be wise to brainstorm a bit about Nepal's peace zone proposal. King Birendra proposed this in the Non-aligned summit in Algiers in 1973 and officially, requested all the nations to accept it. But India disapproved this proposal showing the reason as it contradicts Nepal-India Treaty of 1950.[50]

After 70 years of its signing by outgoing last Rana Prime Minister Mohan Shumser, there has not been single amendment into it. To address several requests from Nepal's establishment and the people, both the governments agreed to form their Eminent Persons Group (EPG) to suggest recommendations into it. The joint EPG has already completed the reports but the respective governments are

49. Yubaraj Ghimirey, *Oli ko China Bhraman: Abasar ki Palayan,* June 18, 2018, https://deshsanchar.com/2018/06/18/66699/
50. Bhattarai, Umesh K., *Conflict to Peace: Transition in Nepal,* New Delhi: Adarsh Books, 2014, p. 20.

reluctant to accept it. Till date, there is no sign to response positively from both the governments but unofficially, the signals are negative at the public forums.

With such mindsets, the stability is far away in this region. Whatever the public wants - it is not necessary for the leaders to follow; they just have to pay attention to strategists on how they can promote their national interest. Nepal's national interest is always compromised by the leaders to fulfill their vested interest from its history.

Nepal's Contemporary Democracies

Nepal entered to open democracy after 1950. But still, it could not stabilize the politics due to bifurcated interests of the power centres. Politics did not remain pure in Nepal. It is rightly said:

> *Democracies can die with a coup d'état or they can die slowly. This happens most deceptively when in piecemeal fashion, with the election of an authoritarian leader, the abuse of governmental power and the complete repression of the opposition ...*[51]

In most contemporary democracies where the system has plunged, the cases are similar as like-minded leaders follow the models that apparently look popular but in reality, they are different. In the recent past, we have seen some rulers who broke the existing system and imposed authoritarian rule as they like. The example could be of General Augusto Pinochet of Chile and President Recep Erdogan of Turkey.

Similarly, Russian President Putin's atrocity to suppress the opponents and its leaders as well as to suspicious poisoning of the close rivals is few other examples. President Donald Trump's suspension of many democratic moves of the predecessors ignoring global concerns in the name of "America First" is not only ridiculous, but also, the reasons of the establishment of the United Nations are in question. His national security advisers' contempt of the International Criminal Court against its ruling of abuse of power of the US Army in Afghanistan that caused genocide has serious concern for the UN Security Council.

How an apex body can function effectively if its founder itself criticizes the United Nations? This is a serious question to restore international peace in the wake of a destabilized world order. Likewise, President Xi Jinping approved for lifetime assignment by the Communist Party of China. In fact, the whole world has similar trend to get into the regime first, and then capture it for long. The

51. Lavitsky, Steven and Zimlatt, Daniel, *How Democracies Die,* New York: Penguin Books, 2018

case of medium and small countries has no difference. The examples can be taken of Venezuela, Philippines, Syria, North Korea including countries of Europe like Hungary, Poland, Austria, and Nepal is no exception.

There is the tendency of the political leaders in the developing countries that once they are elected—they presume as lifetime boss of the citizens, and legitimacy to rule haphazardly. There are many who believe legitimacy is not a one-time event conferred through an election or the establishment of charismatic authority but a continuous process of deepening and broadening the rights and obligations of citizenship.[52]

But in fact, the validation or renewal of public mandate through periodical elections is mandatory to confirm democratic commitment of the political parties and its leaders. The legitimacy that rest on electoral validation is based on zero-sum game with clear winners who rule over the others,[53] but where the citizenries are not well-educated and sincere to use their voting rights—the chances of wrong candidate to win are more. In such a case, people's right to reject or recall system needs to be developed to ensure democracy functioning properly.

How do democracies die? It is a burning question all over the world. Inspired to answer this; Steven Levitsky and Daniel Ziblatt wrote a book in 2018 where they identified many things to answer it. The political institutions are under threat in developing countries. In Nepal, the case is similar as they are captured by gangsters as how mostly the regimes are captured in Africa. The leaders of such gangsters have little or no political knowledge to run the political parties. As what Levitsky and Ziblatt stated about how an authoritative rule overrides democracy is firstly through the rejective ideology to democratic rules of the game.

After the Maoist party entered into mainstream politics, it established a culture to play with the sentiments of the mass, intimidate and terrorize who deny their ideology and capture the regime through the ballots. Left extremists could forge alliance for elections motivated to capture regime; after forming the government, it started ignoring the legitimate opponent and its voice in the parliament.

Despite increased crimes like rape and murder, state sponsored smuggling of precious metals and government failing to investigate them properly and

52. Ghani, Asraf and Lockhart, Clare, *Fixing Failed States:* Oxford University Press, 2008. P-8.
53. Ibid.

bringing the culprits behind the bar. Similarly, the ruling party is busy enough to curtail the civil liberties through new penal code against media, doctors and other professionals. These are the behaviours of the present left government in Nepal that indicate its authoritarian attitude against the rule of the democracy.

Civil-Military Relations

Study of civil-military relation is crucial to understand the entire dynamics of stability in Nepal. Before Nepal's integration, it was divided in many principalities having its own military with unique management. The warlords used to be the sectarian military commanders with authority to levy tax, ensure security and look after the day-to-day administration. They had to pay annual grants to the king. Small-scale skirmishes were very common between or among the principalities as well.

To consolidate divided powers—King Prithvi Narayan Shah from small principality of Gorkha formed a small military that turn to the Nepal Army after its integration. So, King Prithvi Narayan is the founder of present Nepal Army and credit for the establishment of modern Nepal, solely goes to him. The history of Nepal is the proof that identifies the Nepal Army was exclusively formed and groomed for this cause and the contribution of King Prithvi Narayan is no less. Rulers like Bahadur Shah, Rajendra Laxmi, Bhimsen Thapa and Jung Bahadur modernized it and faced internal as well as external threat against Nepal.

Military was absolute means of administration to render public goods at that time. The separate civil service was not introduced; rather civil servants were created just to support military commanders to manage state affairs. The influential and attractive elites who could dominate the others were picked up by the palace and awarded ranks depending upon their loyalty and commitment to them. Those who opposed the palace were tagged traitors—hence confiscated their whole property and forced to go on exile. Few who used to be severely critical were executed either openly to terrorize the mass or poisoned to silent their voice.

The concrete milestone of distinct civil and military services started only after the first popular revolution in 1951. This was the timeline that ended the Rana autocratic family rule and entered into the democratic practices. The transition was not only too long but it reversed to another type of autocracy in 1960 when King Mahendra arrested the democratically elected prime minister through military might.

The country again fell to one party Panchayat system under absolute rule of monarchy supported by the Nepal Army. The civil supremacy was crashed by the military at the very beginning of its democracy. The civil-military relations were further strained when the Nepali Congress was banned and tagged "anti-national elements". Due to state repression, the Nepali congress leaders had to go on exile in India from where they started armed insurgency against the Panchayat system.

The democratic forces toppled the Panchayat system in 1989-90 and established a multi-party based parliamentary system through the second revolution. The constitution of 1990 provisioned the king as the constitutional monarchy having military link intact as supreme commander of Nepal Army. As they had historical connection to each other, the democratic government could not practically bring the Nepal Army under civilian control. In fact, the constitutional provision itself was the hurdle to bring Nepal Army under the democratic government.

The party leaders in the government failed to own the guardianship of the army from the very beginning. They considered it as rival and made unpleasant remarks time and again. They had neither a plan to restructure and reform nor to build a trust to own them. They could have managed better control of the army through the National Security Council having majority of their own and its recommendation mandatory to the king.

Lack of their vision was clearly noticed when PM Girija Prasad Koirala could not mobilize the Nepal Army to rescue bulk of the captured Nepal Police personnels by the Maoist at its initial stage of insurgency. Due to the government's inability, the Nepal Army was more aloof and independent. The relations further worsened when the elected government of the Nepali Congress decided to establish the Nepal Armed Police Force at par with the Nepal Army to crash the burning issue of Maoist insurgency in 2001.

The tussle between the elected government and the Nepal Army surfaced at the highest elevation when the prime minister failed to mobilize it and resigned from the post showing the cause of its reluctance to deploy against the burgeoning insurgency. The cause of the debate could be any, but the relations between the monarchy and the government was also not cordial. The monarchy as the supreme commander of the army could have played a positive role to pacify the tussle between the army and the government for the betterment of the country. But PM G. P. Koirala did not do that - so his role is also controversial in this regard.

The Maoist insurgency was the acid test for the Nepal Army to deliver the mandate of the civilian government after its long interval of major involvement in the insurgency battle after 1960. It was deployed in a limited role to disarm the *Khampa* insurgency in 1973. The *Khampa* used Nepal's territory as a sanctuary to launch insurgency operations in Tibet. In fact, the Nepal Army has always cooperated with the government unless the interests of its military commander have not clashed with each other.

Let us examine the case of Puspa Kamal Dahal's resignation episode as the prime minister of Nepal. The case has link with the then Chief of the Army Staff (COAS) General Rookmangad Katawal's interest to prolong his tenure through an amendment of his date of birth. The case was under trial at the Supreme Court for almost three years with several hearings that were postponed. Army Headquarters under the COAS General Katwal was reluctant to submit his personal records to the court.[54]

Next in the line of command, Lieutenant General Kul Bahadur Khadka was eager to take over once the verdict of the court would have granted in his favour—and it was quite natural. But the things did not move as he wished. Most suspected that General Katwal manipulated the court for postponing the hearing dates till he retired as per the new date of birth. The court later cancelled the writ petition showing that the cause as convicted have already retired. It did not feel necessary to establish precedence against any wrong doers in the future.

Having full background picture of the army, a decade long rival Maoist was waiting for the opportunity to discredit and dismantle it. Denial to take part in a national sports event where Maoist's Young Communist League (YCL) wanted to represent as the national team by the army and for few other reasons—PM Dahal decided to dismiss General Katwal from the post of the COAS. This led to a controversy in the government and ultimately the then President Ram Baran Yadav had to intervene to allow General Katwal to continue as the COAS of the Nepal Army.

This was the most confrontational period of the civil-military relations in the modern history of Nepal. Let's examine another case, the Ranamukteshwor

54. Op.cit. Bhattarai, Umesh K., *Conflict to Peace: Transition in Nepal,* New Delhi: Adarsh Books, 2014, p. 118-119.

incident during an infant King Griban Yuddha's rule—his father Rana Bahadur Shah was killed by his step-brother. The situation was seized by Bhimsen Thapa from which he emerged to power as the "de-facto" ruler of Nepal. He was civilian turn to military ruler who had neither a professional training nor had fought a single war. As it was fully a military dominated regime, though Thapa was purely a civilian became a brutal military commander afterwards.

The next significant event in the civil-military relations was the *Kot* massacre which enabled Jung Bahadur Rana to emerge as a military general to coup against the regime and grab the state power from the queen, who had the attorney rights from her incompetent King Rajendra Bikram Shah. The last royal massacre in which King Birendra and his family were killed helped emerged King Gyanendra to power, but who had waged this is still not clear. These ill-fated historical events are the examples of Nepal's instability that have deep-rooted impact in its political leaders and the society at large.

In the contemporary events, the Nepal Army was formed, organized and groomed in the autocratic set-up. Family centric officer's corps mainly commanded the rural hill-based soldiers with less educational background. They have no or little ambitions as they mostly face hand to mouth problems at home. With such background, they were not in a position to complaint to elite English-speaking high-class officers in the past. These officers used to consider the political leaders inferior to them in education, exposure and knowledge having no practical experience to run the state effectively. At the other, the political leaders had an impression that all the generals and the officers that have feudal orientation are corrupt and exploited the soldiers, have little education and talk high to show that they are superior. With these mindsets at the both ends weakened complimentary growth of the civil-military relations in the past.

At the present scenario, these mindsets are gradually changing in the political as well as in the military relations. The military commanders are trained in democratic set-up where the military is groomed to support the civilian authority. So, the Nepal Army is not confrontational to civilian authority, but it has dangerous coalition for corruption with them. This interest coincides with all in Nepal who has authority to mobilize state resources. It is understood worldwide—authority is abused by those who have power. The constitutional provision to curb corruption is faulty as all the constitutional heads, ministers, military and judiciary are waived to trial by the Commission for Investigation of Abuse of Authority (CIAA).

The military needs to be professional to discharge their duty tasked by the constitution. Professionalism does not only suffice to a good training and highly equipped army, but also, demands a firm loyalty towards the people and the democratic system mandated by the very people itself. They should be well-paid and their welfare must be well looked after by the government. A corruption free system can only create an environment conducive to stability. In Nepal, its stability is diluted in the grave interest of corruption to embezzle public money irrespective of ranks, files and services.

Chapter Four

Disgusting Nepali Politics

Politics Impurity

The *Mahabharata* is an epic in the *Sanatan Hindu* mythology that teaches us the reality behind the politics. Why politics is not pure? The answer is like the way it is dealt with power - it does not remain at one place forever. The tendency of power is to shift to those who can absorb it. The power neither sees who is ethical or not, nor by what means it is achieved—just shifts who can hold it. In one sense, politics is the science of power which cannot be achieved without capturing the regime. That is why the politicians make groups—sub-groups and manipulate the system bargaining for power with the powerful. Mergers, splits and conversions take place when politicians lack power in the existing circumstances.

Power hungriness in politics up to this point is quite natural but seldom it crosses the limit when there starts blackmailing, kidnapping, intimidation, terrorism and killings to grab power. The *Mahabharata* epic deals all about power hungriness to regime capturing. The present political culture is guided by such a philosophy that establishes the saying as "politics is always impure". Let us examine this by analyzing the various facets as the Nepali politics is disgusting instead of several attempts to purify it.

Geopolitical Constraints

Politics fall into the wider domain of the entire societal study, where human development carries an important role to play. Stability and development are complimentary to each other. Geopolitics is the study of geography and politics analyzing their relativity to find out their strategic value in the specific sphere. The connectivity and infrastructure developments help strategic movement of the people and resources that dictate geopolitical constraints as such. So, geopolitics is not static rather changes with the relative factors like connectivity and developments.

Based on the geopolitical constraints of the specific location in the prevailing situation—its strength and weakness are accessed. Understanding it as knowledge is equally important to negotiate with other powers. Failing to do so—the weak has to face negative consequences. For example, Nepal has been punished several times in its history when its leaders failed to know geopolitical constraints of this country very well. They also failed to follow it as a discipline to make lifestyle easy. Their grave negligence was to ignore the importance of connectivity that can only negotiate geopolitical constraints at large. Signing of the "Belt and Road Initiative" with China and the decision to open access to its ports is Nepal's first step to open connectivity towards the north. Once these avenues are open - Nepal's geopolitical dynamics will automatically change.

Nepal is surrounded by three nuclear powers of Asia—needs a careful policy to adopt as to whom to align with. The policy of non-alignment has no value in present context—so where Nepal wants to incline for its betterment is a burning question.[55] The Tibet factor for Nepal was always critical from its history. From the time of John F. Kennedy as Bruce Riedel described in his book *JFK's Forgotten Crisis*, that CIA dropped 29,000 pounds of equipment, enough arms and ammunitions for 400 Tibetan rebels and ample number of graduates from the Colorado base into Mustang of Nepal.[56] Of course, the Nepal Army was deployed to destroy them later, but this is the evidence that Nepal was used as a sanctuary to the armed rebellion against China. So, Nepal must understand the disciplinary prospect of the geopolitical constraints to be responsive to avoid direct confrontations with the neighbours.

Open Border Legacy

The Indo-Nepal border is open and poorly regulated for long due to Nepal's inability to fence it and local politicians wrangling to fulfil their vested interest beyond the border. Before the Indo-Nepal Friendship Treaty of 1950, the British East India Company was reluctant to keep the border secured, so that Nepal remains fragile. This would have allowed them to draw out natural resources like timber, minerals and manpower for its force to fight at another front. Nepal's autocratic rulers were focussed to embezzle public property rather than spending to regulate the border.

55. Bhattarai, Umesh K. (2018) New Media and Its Role in Stabilizing Nepal: A Geopolitical Context (eds) in Media Diplomacy and its evolving role in the current geopolitical climate. IGI Publishers, USA. P.39.
56. Riedel, Bruce, 2016. *JFK's Forgotten Crisis,* New Delhi: HarperCollins. P. 61.

Showing the cause of geopolitical compulsions, India trapped Nepal's outgoing Rana Prime Minister Mohan Shumsher to sign the 1950 Treaty that institutionalized "open border" thereafter. It is learnt that the recent Eminent Persons Group from Nepal has insisted on regulating open border and many other issues but the handing over of this report is pending due to the reluctance of Indian PM Narendra Modi and of Nepal's PM K. P. Sharma Oli which may bring failure to the grand design. If it happens so, then the "open border" will remain at the status quo—discouraging entire Nepalis and to fuel an "anti-India" feeling again in Nepal. The repeated embargo will have minimal impact to the people living near the open border but for the hill people it is hard to survive.

The demand of trade diversification is high among the hill people who want to enhance connectivity and trade at the Northern frontier. The people at the Tarai and Indians living in Southern part mostly advocate "open border" as a compulsion due to traditional socio-cultural ties. There are some who believe that "open border" is must from an economic sustainability point of view. "*Roti Beti ka sawal*" means the people cannot sustain at the border if it is closed because their livelihood is based on *"edhar ka mal udhar"* – in honest language it is smuggling in another sense. In my response to the *Foreign Policy Research Centres (FPRC)*, New Delhi, Journal 19[57] on the consequences of transforming an open to a close border; Nepal and India are blaming each other for its inability to control illicit trade, fake currency smuggling, cross-border terrorism and money laundering. Both have realised as it should be regulated at least the as many as 500 to 1000 bicyclists that uses each custom point to smuggle petty household items everyday. The taxes that could have been collected are spoilt as they do not come to the government system. It is more harmful to the Nepali side as production of even the consumer items are rampant due to the weak industrial as well as export base.

Weak Security Cognition

The general understanding of security is poor in Nepal. The British impression of the Nepalis as brave is mostly upheld at the West. Bravery and intelligentsia have rivalry between them. An intelligent generally calculates advantage and disadvantage, profit and loss, good or bad before doing anything. Bravery is basically related to loyalty and honesty and bit foolish in calculating advantage

57. Bhattarai, Umesh Kumar. *India-Nepal Relations*-Foreign Policy Research Center, New Delhi India, Journal 19, 2014 P. 76. http://www.fprc.in/Pragya-NEPAL-19.pdf

and disadvantage, profit and loss and good and bad while discharging duties. Such personalities are highly motivated and devoted for the cause. Pride and recognition by the parental organization is precious for them.

In the mid of the Anglo-Nepal War (1814-16), the British East India Company started deserters and fresh Nepali youths recruiting in its army to weaken Nepal.[58] The war was devastating and had long-term effect on Nepal's future military expansion. The territorial loss incurred serious financial blow to Nepal. The British were successful to weaken as it would never again constitute a threat to their hegemony on the sub-continent.[59] This enabled the British attitude as a sole determination to decide Nepal's image at the international arena. It was due to the British assessment of the fighting capabilities of the Gorkha soldiers who fought most heroically during the war and had exhibited superb fighting qualities.[60]

Prime Minister Jung Bahadur who took it as a grave British design to play with the Nepali nationalism, issued an order to confiscate the entire property who defies the state's order. Jagadish Sharma in his book *Nepal: Struggle for Existence* agreed that initially such recruitments before the war were limited in nature. But after his demise, his brothers like Bir and Chandra Sumsher wholeheartedly allowed the British to recruit Gorkha soldiers in its army. After the independence of India in 1947, it also opted to continue recruitment as did the British through the Tripartite Treaty. Then onwards, Nepali youths are used as mercenaries in foreign armies.

The leaders in the democratic setup did not dare to challenge the hegemonic influence of the powerful nations. The British legacy in Nepal's bureaucracy and politicians' circle is so deep-rooted that it still has not gone after almost 70 years of democratic practice. India is severely affected by such mindsets being directly ruled under colonial framework compared to Nepal. The way British used to impose its will-India too, wanted to establish a similar hegemonic influence from the very beginning of its independence. In the changed environment, Nepal does not want such imposition - so confrontations were frequent from the time of

58. Bhattarai, Umesh K. (2018) *Demography Changes and Threat on National Security*- A paper presentation (eds) in Bharat-Nepal Relations: Defense and Security Issues. Neeti Anusandhan Pratisthan. Nepal (NeNAP). P-113.
59. Sharma, Jagadish. (2006). Nepal: Struggle for Existence. Comnlnc, ICT Private Ltd, Kathmandu, Nepal. P-7.
60. Ibid.

first transition to democracy in 1950 till today. There were declared as well as undeclared economic embargos many times to Nepal. The British exercised direct hegemony and control over Nepal's natural resources after the independence of India has gradually decreased but still deployed Gorkha troops and its retirees as a tool to earn commissions from the Gorkha Reserve Unit deployed to guard the royalties in Brunei Darussalam.[61]

The case does not end with the British alone to in exploiting Nepal's human resources, India too opted the similar path like that of the British to re-employ Ex- Indian Gorkhas along with regular Gorkha forces during the visit of its former Vice President Mohammad Hamid Ansari to Brunei in 2016.[62] But the dilemma is that the Government of Nepal has not revealed any news pertaining to the re-employment of the Gorkha troops and its retirees at the official capacity. The brokering of human resources and embezzling commissions out of re-employment of Nepal's muscle power elsewhere is purely demoralizing its nationhood in the present context.

Nepal's diplomatic capacity to promote its national interest had been openly undermined when Vice President Hamid proposed the royalties of Brunei for the service of the Indian Gorkha Regiments if they agreed upon the condition.[63] The points were continuously raised to respective governments if they want the Gorkha troops directly from the Government of Nepal rather than re-employing from other sources like India and the British Governments. The volunteers and the retirees from the Nepal Army were offered to the Brunei Government in 1985 by the Government of Nepal. It could not materialise due to the undercover meddling by the British and the Indian establishments. The case was mired upon the disgusted politics which was not clear about how to manage the British and the Indian hegemony in this regard. So, as the Government of Nepal has opted to review the 1950 Treaty with India - it should also expedite reviewing the 1947 Tripartite Treaty with Britain and India regarding the Gorkha recruitments.

This is not all about Nepal's security sector mismanagement. The corruption cases related to the security forces are in the headlines in the national newspapers

61. Marszal, Andrew. (2016). *India offers to send its Gurkhas to Brunei.* The Telgraph. https://www.telegraph.co.uk/news/worldnews/asia/india/12137906/Indian-Gurkhas-could-soon-replace-British-forces-in-Brunei.ht
62. Ibid.
63. Poudel, Purusottam. (2016). Khumchido Antarrastriya Saakh. *Annapurna Post Daily.* Kathmandu. http://annapurnapost.com/news/61574

almost daily. Investigation of such reports and prosecution are poor. Ministers, constitutional heads, judiciary and military are waived from such investigations and trials by the Commission for the Investigation of Abuse of Authority (CIAA) through the constitutional provision. But the constitution does not waive such trials and prosecutions after retirement of these public service holders at all. Or, the Government of Nepal can dismiss the service and bring into the public hearing of such cases to trial and prosecute at the court.

The dilemma is the corruption has become a normal culture and institutionalized at all levels of the bureaucracy and political parties. If we see the list of Inspector General of Nepal Police Force in the last decade, there are none who had not been punished on the charge for corruption by the court. The case is similar with the Nepal Armed Police Force. The corruption allegations are reported heavily against the Chief of the Army Staffs of the Nepal Army but not a single case is filed to any of the retired generals at the court. Generally, no political leaders want to take a risk going against the military establishment as they are corrupt themselves. It is reported that no security chiefs get appointment without paying a ransom amount to the concerned government heads. The professional efficiency, competency and loyalty are compromised in lieu of financial gains. In such milieu, the security chiefs cannot be expected to work effectively - to promote and preserve the national interest of the country.

Political Wrangling - Misfortune for Stability

Nepali politics is mired up with selfish desires of the third grade leaders who have neither long-term vision nor the willpower to implement the programmes and projects of the public needs. They are graded third because the first grade youths very seldom join politics, the second-grade reaches to a level to lead but compromises ideology in lieu of financial gains, so their image get faded in the crowds; the third-grade have neither the ideology nor the integrity. They represent gangsters and encourage criminology in the politics. They control the entire system under their grip through wealth, woman and weapon (3W). In other words, they capture the regime through populist slogans initially, and later, impose autocracy gradually.

Due to the acute poverty, illiteracy and exploitation of the autocratic regime—the people misunderstood and misread the politics. They failed to distinguish who is wrong and who is right due to the confusion the mainstream parties and their leaders created in their minds. The third-grade leaders as mentioned above embezzled property through corruption; captured regime and imposed autocracy - a new form of oligarchy. The electoral system is manipulated to suit their own cadres and group to be elected officially. Political alliances are made to trap vote banks. The party activists use all the coercive tactics to block rivals to cast votes against their party. Apparently, the overall process looks democratic and liberal as well as populist, but from the depth—the entire system supports groups, nepotism and favouritism.

Nepal was trapped by such autocratic rule from 17th century onwards. The Kathmandu valley was the nerve centre for its civilization, economic activities and cultural development. Before Prithvi Narayan's rule, it was under *Nepal Mandal*—a union of *Malla Newar* rulers who used to administer the entire valley affairs of Kathmandu, Bhaktapur and Lalitpur, collectively. After Nepal's unification at the East and the West, the Kathmandu Durbar could not administer the state as before. The expansion of the territory was quite faster but Nepali states' presence at the local level was poor. As a result, the Shah Rulers gradually lost popularity outside the Kathmandu valley. In fact, the civil rights of the citizens were poor but the military expansion remained the priority.

This was the time when the British East India Company was consolidating power in the South and Imperial China was tightening its grip in the North. The wave of Soviet expansion under its new communist regime was invading towards Central Asia. It was expected from them to capture Tibet and enter Nepal threatening the British in India. The Imperial Chinese regime in Beijing was quite worried of their move in this part of the world. In such threat perception, Nepal was compelled to restructure its military and equip adequately. The growing military expenses at that time compelled the regime to compromise civil works and economic developments of the country. Up to this point could be justifiable but palace embezzlement for luxurious life as indicated by the historians discredit the Shah Rulers after King Prithvi Narayan.

With many ups and downs in palace centric politics, ultimately Nepal involved fighting with Tibet supported by China in 1792 and with the East India Company in 1814-16. The last Anglo-Nepal war was the turning point of its expansion. In fact, Nepal lost this battle so heavily that its sovereignty, freedom of action and independence were always in question thereafter. There are some intellectuals who do not agree with this opinion but this is a reality that we have to accept. It was in the middle of the battle in 1815 when the British offered the Nepali youths to join their army with lucrative salary and benefits compared to the Nepal Government. King Ranjit Singh of Independent Punjab did the same. In fact, the Nepali palace failed to honour war heroes who contributed wholeheartedly sacrificing their lives to expand Nepal. The Palace was actually embroiled with conspiracy of its courtiers and generals. It was Bhimsen Thapa, a self declared prime-minister and commander-in-chief who had never been a professional soldier led a war in his whim. The sole blame of the defeat of the war and the plunging of the nation into a deep crisis led him to detention and later, forced suicide in custody.

Next to Bhimsen Thapa who emerged in power as de-facto to the Shah Rulers was Jung Bahadur Rana. He also became a powerful prime minister through bloodshed as Thapa. The difference was that Jung Bahadur was a professional soldier, more charismatic and more of a diplomat than Bhimsen Thapa. He was clever and power hungry. He knew the geopolitics of entire South Asia and Nepal's position in conversance to emerging British power in the region. Just a day after the *Kot* massacre from which he seized the state power—visited the British resident early morning in Kathmandu to have blessings as the next powerful ruler of Nepal.

The British resident who had ignored the audience to King Rajendra Bikram the previous night when *Kot* massacre was going on—recognized Jung Bahadur immediately the next morning as a powerful prime minister. Perhaps, it was the impact of indecisiveness of the palace on matters related to British proposals and a part of a coercive diplomacy to ease decisions through a single autocratic ruler who can decide independently. Jung Bahadur later proved himself as the most competent, trustworthy and capable leader of his time in the Nepali history.

After Jung Bahadur's death, his brothers assumed the power but none of them proved competent to his level. But they remained faithful to the British. They provided military support to the allied forces in the World War I and II. They even contributed a covert force to launch clandestine operations against the Boxer rebellion in Tibet.[64] The rebellion was against the Chinese Qing dynasty by the Tibetan elites.

64. In 1900, in what became known as the Boxer Rebellion (or the Boxer Uprising), a Chinese secret organization called the Society of the Righteous and Harmonious Fists led an uprising in northern China against the spread of Western and Japanese influence there. The Qing dynasty, established in 1644, was weakened by the Boxer Rebellion. Following an uprising in 1911, the dynasty came to an end and China became a republic in 1912. https://www.history.com/topics/china/boxer-rebellion

The British supported the authoritative Rana rulers with a hope to exploit natural resources of Nepal. In fact, they did not capture Nepal considering its geopolitical location that would have led them to direct confrontation with imperial China, so they better preferred it to leave buffer. After Jung Bahadur, the Nepali politics was under their grip as the Ranas were their puppet and were easy to suppress the illiterate and poor people through them. This way Nepal was under a de-facto British rule from the time of the Anglo-Nepal War (1814-16). The British abandoned India in 1947 with its legacy to trap as much as before. There are several issues that were still unsolved in South Asia as the hot bed between two nuke states, India and Pakistan. In respect to Nepal, the Union of India and its leaders continued the British policy with new a treaty of Friendship in 1950. It was more or less a continuation of the Anglo-Nepal Sughauli Treaty in 1816. The Treaty on the tripartite Gorkha Recruitment among Nepal-Britain and India in 1947 was also the continuation of the previous treaties. By this way, the Nepali youths were made mercenaries eroding its nationalism till today.

Weak Nepali State in the Present Context

With such history, the Nepali nationhood was developed in an autocratic setup. The Shah rulers were again restored under the Indian grand design after the British abandonment in 1947. The awakening of democracy and independence in Asia and Africa from the colonial rule insisted the Nepalis to raise a voice against the autocratic Ranas. It was the Indian PM Jawaharlal Nehru who is said to design a plot to seek asylum by King Tribhuvan and his family in New Delhi. There are few intellectuals who claim as king himself did not seek any asylum rather he was kidnapped by the Indian establishment to bargain with Rana PM Mohan Shumsher to make a fresh deal with Nepal. People suspect that the 1950 Treaty is the outcome of that deal. Hence, leaders like Dr. K. I. Singh did not accept Delhi settlement and his resentment led him to exile in Beijing. Due to Indian wrangling in the Nepali politics from the very beginning of its independent – the relations could not become as cordial as it ought to be.

The Indian leaders copied the British legacy to deal with the Nepali leaders after their independence. In the battle with the British for freedom, the Nepali leaders on exile supported the Indian nationalist leaders and fought against the British. But after the independence, their attitude to look upon the Nepali leaders changed. They became more selfish to exploit Nepal's natural resources for which they supported to liberate it from the Rana autocrats. This attitude spread anti-India feelings in Nepal from the very outset of its independence.

The British policy was to contain Nepal in spite of capturing it so as to refrain from the liabilities it had to bear as the governing regime. In other words, it preferred Nepal to remain a buffer but loyal to its system. After the Indian independence in 1947, PM Nehru also advocated the British policy to leave Nepal as it was. But then influential Home Minister Sardar Vallab Bhai Patel was against his policy and strongly opined to annex Nepal into its union. Pondicherry which was under French control was easily liberated but Goa under Portugal was resisted primarily.[65] Kashmir was the hot cake since it had been annexed in 1947—on which issue India has already fought three wars with Pakistan. Till date, the regular skirmishes are going on in the international border between India and Pakistan. In fact, the dispute is so deep-rooted as the demand of the plebiscite is not only pending since 1948 on which the UN Security Council had issued a resolution into it. Modi Government has scrapted the special status that was granted to the Kashmiries under the Article 370 and 35 A of the Indian Constitution.

Kashmir is divided in two parts threatening the entire South Asian stability from the time of India-Pakistan partisan in 1947. Imagine what could have been if Nepal would also have annexed into the Union of India as Kashmir? Today Nepal is fragile and its economic development is not as its two big neighbours. In addition, its stability is jeopardized. At times, the scholars raise questions as Nepal is now only fragile or it is really heading towards a failed state. Why it is fragile and heading towards a failed state? It is a burning question for social scientists to draw a framework of research in the international security and stability of South Asia.

Asia Pacific Vs Indo-Pacific Strategy in Nepali Political Discourse

After China's strengthened its interest to revive the old silk-road to link modern trade and commerce with the enhanced geo-strategic advantages, it has challenged other international powers, respectively. Four strategic manoeuvres in the name of the Belt and Road Initiative (BRI) also known as One Belt One

65. India used force on December 20, 1961 to liberate Goa from the hands of Portugal. It was against PM Nehru's philosophy to settle all international disputes by peaceful means. He had intervened with force to keep Kashmir a part of India in 1947 (As revealed by Bruce Reidel in his book 'JFK's Crisis', published in 2015, p-74).

Road (OBOR) connecting mainland China with rest of the world stimulated suspicion on its intension.

South Asia, a homeland of India, an immediate and powerful neighbour of China with whom it had fought a major war in 1962 and has been facing instant resistance at the border in Aksai Chin and Arunanchal Pradesh is critical about its BRI project. Despite the criticism, Nepal, Bangladesh, Pakistan, Sri Lanka, and Maldives have already accepted BRI and Bhutan is said to be in process, at the same time India is sponsoring new connectivity approach as three regional blocs such as Bangladesh, Bhutan, India and Myanmar (BBIM), Bangladesh, Bhutan, India and Nepal (BBIN) and Bangladesh, China, India and Myanmar (BCIM). In all the blocs, Bangladesh and India are made a common partner. The prime motives for being a member of the regional blocs are essentially to have economy at the centre and politics at strategy.[66] BIMSTEC is another cooperation founded in 1997 to enhance connectivity by the Indian establishment where Nepal is a member.

Image-1

Routes of the China-proposed Belt and Road Initiative

Although there are many regional blocs and sub-blocs where Nepal is a member, the Indo-Pacific is more or less a substitute to the Asia-Pacific geographical region after President Trump became the 45th president of USA in 2017. It was designed to isolate China from the rest of the countries in Asia, America, and Australia surrounded by the Pacific and the Indian Ocean. This new concept has been suspiciously accepted by India as what Rahul Roy

66. India must watch Chinese plans when opting between BBIM & BCIM- a paper of Observer Research Foundation, https://www.orfonline.org/research/india-must-watch-chinese-plans-when-opting-between-bbim-bcim/

Choudhury wrote as India's "inclusive Indo-Pacific policy seeks to balance relations with the US and China".[67] He further writes unlike the US policy; PM Modi's vision seeks partnership with ASEAN and continued engagement with China. He quoted Michael D. Swaine who elaborated that in President Trump's "free and open Indo-Pacific (FOIP)" India and Japan are poorly suited to serve as the anchors of an Indo-Pacific strategic domain and other Asian states would likely resist taking sides in a polarising Manichean contest between China and the United States.[68]

In the wake of President Xi Jinping's pending high level visit for the last two years (which concluded recently) and international meddling into it, the USA has proposed Nepal to become a part of its "Indo-Pacific" team to counter BRI. A Ran Bin University Scholar Dr. Rupak Sapkota in his article published in the Kantipur Daily on January 24, 2019[69] reveals this fact, which was initially concealed by the Minister of Foreign Affairs, Mr. Pradeep Kumar Gyawali. Speaking at a media briefing immediately after the US visit - he mentioned that he and his counterpart Michael Pompeo discussed a host of issues related to the "Indo-Pacific" but no such strategy.[70] In fact, the Nepal Communist Party led government is not really clear how to deal with the US proposal that is directed to counter the BRI that the Oli Government has already signed. The Quadrilateral Security Dialogue (QSD also known as QUAD)[71] has designed this strategy during the military exercise in Malabar. As USA and other member partners, India is not excited, Dr. Sapkota mentioned in his article.

Communist Connection Vs Indo-Pacific Strategy

After the foreign minister's visit to the USA in December 2018, the issue of Indo-Pacific has intensely surfaced in the Nepali politics. Although USA had used Nepal's weak polity and its administrative mechanism to foul play in Tibet against China since its annexation in 1950, it has lots of ups and downs as well.

67. https://www.iiss.org/blogs/analysis/2018/07/india-inclusive-indo-pacific-policy-china-relations
68. http://carnegieendowment.org/2018/03/02/creating-unstable-asia-u.s.-free-and-open-indo-pacific-strategy-pub-75720
69. नेपाल चीन कि अमेरिकातिर- ttps://www.kantipurdaily.com/opinion/2019/01/24/1548295 42119824417.html
70. 'Nepal Not part of Indo-Indo Pacific Strategy' The Himalayan Times, December 24, 2018. https://thehimalayantimes.com/nepal/nepal-not-part-of-indo-pacific-strategy/
71. An informal strategic dialogue partnership among USA, Japan, Australia and India initiated by Japanese PM Shinzo Abe in 2007.

USA had even requested for the mediation of the Nepal Communist Party leaders to play a significant role to stabilise the Korean peninsula.[72] Perhaps, the way the Nepal Communist Party led government had sponsored the Asia Pacific Summit of the Universal Peace Federation programme which has parental connection with South Korea inspired the US to stabilise the Korean peninsula through its influential leaders. On the contrary, as every coin has two sides—the US might have realised later that the communist connection could also be used against it by China to derail the "Indo-Pacific" strategy in Nepal. The Venezuelan connection of the Nepal Communist Party and its co-chair's statement against the US bloc needs empirical analysis to find out the communist connection with the Indo-Pacific strategy in particular.

The 1960s was the peak of the US intervention in Tibet during the John F. Kennedy's presidential period. Mustang of Nepal was heavily used as an administrative base and training camp to launch insurgency inside Tibet.[73] Upon Chinese request, the Nepal Army had crashed the base and captured the camp. Due to such incident in the past, the Chinese authority is still suspicious of the US manoeuvre in Nepal. In 2001, the royal regime in Nepal deported 18 Tibetans to the Chinese authority who were arrested while illegally passing through to go to Dharmasala in India. The human rights body was opposed to this. The US and other Western countries advocated for their rights. So, Nepal is trapped in between these world powers to safeguard its sovereignty and keep its independence intact.

Nepal had undergone a decade long insurgency waged by the leftist against the royal regime. Now, this faction is representing the Nepal Communist Party which is in power. By name, it was the Maoist party carrying the Maoist legacy in Nepal. Whether it has link with the Communist Party of China or not - is not proven yet. So, blaming it for unproved allegation will be unfair. The 'Indo-Pacific' strategy of USA will be beneficial for Nepal or not is a separate matter in the national debate.

MCC - a Fresh Debate in Nepal

The politics on Millennuim Challenge Corporation (MCC) is at the peak in

72. United States seeks Nepal's help in resolving Korean peninsula problem- The Himalayan Times, December 25, 2018 https://thehimalayantimes.com/nepal/united-states-seeks-nepals-help-in-resolving-korean-peninsula-problem/
73. Bruce Reidel, JFK's Forgotten Crisis, 2015, p-59

the Nepali political sphere. It has been suspected that it is a part of the United States' "Indo-Pacific Strategy". But appearantly, it looks like an innovation and an independent US foreign assistance agency that is helping lead the fight against global poverty according to what it expresses in its website. The USA provides support to governments that focus on good policies, ownership and results. MCC provides time bound grants promoting economic growth, reducing poverty and strengthening institutions.

But at the other, it has categorically mentioned that it will not only support stability but also, enhance American interest as well. So, we must understand that no country supports through financial aid that they gather from their tax payers perk without their interest is promoted in the host country.

The latest controversy on the then Speaker Krishna Bahadur Mahara's case has been twisted from rape to some other issues once PM K. P. Sharma Oli blamed him in his recent interview in the *Kantipur Daily* that he was reluctant to floor the government's proposal at the parliament to accept MCC worth NRs 50 billion to connect Lapsifedi to Sunouli (300 KM Electric Transmission Line of 400 KV) and to renovate roads on that sector. As Krishna Bahadur Mahara was already blamed to working for China, it looks quite relevant. But another Co-Chair of the Nepal Communist Party supported him through BBC Nepali Service that he alone cannot stop flooring the governments' proposal in the parliament.

Besides, some intelligentsia suspect that it is related to the trans-border electric transmission to India, so its approval is also mandatory. The US Embassy in Kathmandu has also learnt to be insisting for Indian consent into it. But PM Oli did not see any problem on it as India-Nepal has already signed a Power-Purchase Agreement recently. Despite all these, PM Oli has also revealed in the same interview to *Kantipur Daily* that Nepal is not part of the US Indo-Pacific Strategy, so how can he accept financial aid under the MCC, which is designed to promote American interest in the host country? Basically, the entire American interest in the Asia Pacific is guided to promote the Indo-Pacific Strategy after the evolution of Donand Trump as the new US president in 2017. To manage such mindset, it looks quite confusing in our policy to deal with the USA at one side and China at the other. If we fail to manage both the powers tactfully, we may plunge to a problem very soon.

Chapter Five

Period of Total War

Military in Ancient and Medieval Periods

Nepal's military history can be traced from 350 BCE onwards, when the Gopal, Mahispal, Kirat, Licchavi and Malla rulers had their own armies. Archaeological inscriptional evidence indicates the abolition of one dynasty through mass military mobilisation in this era.[74] In 647 CE, King Narendra Dev, the Licchavi ruler of Kathmandu, supported China to invade the Southern Kingdoms with 7000 cavalry and 3500 infantry troops.[75] The case was very serious when a Chinese envoy, Wang-Chhen-Tse, was maltreated by the Indian ruler Harshvardhan of Kannauj, who opted for help both from Nepal and Tibet to launch a punitive expedition.[76] Compared to others, the Licchavi era was much developed and stable in the medieval period.[77] The rulers of that era were influenced by Indian rulers like Chandragupta Maurya, who had 600,000 infantry and 30,000 horse-based and 9,000 elephant-based cavalry to safeguard the Maghad dynasty against the invaders of the West and the North.[78] The Nepali society, whether Hindu, Buddhist or contemporary political ideology, has sprung almost exclusively from India. Moreover, the Nepali political traditions since Emperor Ashoka's time in the fourth century BCE have been closely integrated with those of Northern India.[79] At a later date, the Nepali rulers were also influenced by the powerful Mughals, who had a strong military in between the 16th and early 18th centuries, which inspired them to quell emerging rival powers accordingly.[80]

Available archaeological evidence provides some clues to study the military development from the Licchavi and Malla dynasties of Nepal. At that time, the present-day Nepal was divided into various principalities. The Baisi/Chaubisi

74. Baidya, Tulasi Ram, *Ancient and Medieval Military History of Nepal* (ed.), in *Military History of Nepal* (Part I), Royal Nepal Army Headquarters, 1992, p. 3.
75. Ibid., p. 12.
76. Whelpton, John, *A History of Nepal*, Cambridge University Press, 2015, p. 19.
77. Prof. Dinesh Raj Pant, in an interview with the author in Kathmandu on 7 November 2016.
78. Baidya, *Ancient and Medieval Military History of Nepal*, n. 1, p. 4.
79. Rose, Leo E., *Nepal: Strategy for Survival*, London: University of California Press, 1971, p. 10.
80. Ibid.

states dominated in the West and the Kirats and Limbus were strong in the East. But Kathmandu Valley remained the nerve centre of power, dominating all the surrounding principalities, as it had extensive trade relations with Tibet and the Southern neighbours, including the East India Company.

In the early medieval period, after the Licchavi dynasty, most feudal elites, who were *Kyathnayak* (warlords), had their own army.[81] They used to provide their forces to the state, so there was no need to have a large standing army for any of the tiny states. On the other hand, the Khas Malla rulers of Western Nepal had a competent standing military. Bahadur Shah, who later integrated his kingdom into modern Nepal, also had a credible army. The Khas Magars of Western Nepal were recognised as great warriors even by King Prithvi Narayan Shah. The Karnat kings of Simroungarh in Southern Nepal also had a well-organised standing army.[82]

In the late medieval period, the Khas Mallas, Karnats, the three Malla rulers of Kathmandu Valley and the Sen rulers of east Nepal were powerful. The Mallas of Kathmandu Valley built strategically located forts. King Sri-Niwas Malla of Lalitpur had a stone inscription in the temple of Rato Machhindra Nath tasking his people to build forts, walls and bridges and contribute physically in times of emergency. Defiance of this order was punishable.[83]

In the late medieval period, there was conscription in the Gorkha and Bhaktapur states.[84] Conscription was also adopted by the Malla kings. Later, they opted not to have a standing army but to have a volunteer army. On any strategic gain by the state, members of the army were rewarded with the spoils of victory.[85] An example is the Bhaktapur state, which was under constant aggression by Kathmandu and Laltipur. Bhaktapur state effectively repulsed this aggression by popular participation under Ranajit Malla, who offered attractive rewards to his people for their support.

Military Administration

In the ancient and medieval periods, the king used to be the supreme commander of the army. (This tradition is currently being followed, where the President is

81. Ibid.
82. Ibid., p. 6.
83. Tiwari, Ramji, *Abhilekh Sangrah,* Part 10, Samsodhan Mandal, 1963, pp. 9-10.
84. Baidya, *Ancient and Medieval Military History of Nepal* (ed.), n. 1, p. 7.
85. Rajbamshi, Sankar Man, *An Archaeological Evidence of Inscription from Bhaktapur*, Nepal and Asian Research Centre Report.

the supreme commander of the Nepal Army.) The king decided who should be the army chief and when to launch a war against which state, and conclude a treaty with any other state. The council of ministers and the army chief managed the military affairs on the king's behalf. Military ranks and assignments were conferred by the court on the army chief's recommendation subject to the king's final approval. The rank and portfolio were primarily given on the basis of class and caste rather than on qualification and competence. The army chief was responsible for administering routine affairs, inspecting the forts for war preparedness and for commanding active operations.[86]

In the late medieval period, every household was expected to provide adults to fight for the nation. There was no caste, class, tribal or religious restriction to join the army. But the rulers made their choice of the warrior classes. An example is Prithvi Narayan Shah, who mainly relied on the Khas tribe for his warlike pursuits.[87] The Khas had a history of almost 400 years fighting for the Khas Mallas in Western Nepal. Nevertheless, it took Prithvi Narayan Shah 32 years to conquer the Kathmandu Valley with the Khas as the backbone of his army.[88] Mukund Sen of Palpa also employed Khas Magars twice to attack the Kathmandu Valley, but failed conclusively in the endeavour. Jaya Prakash Malla of Kathmandu in his turn relied mainly on Nagarkoti from Kumaon and Garhwal for his military ventures.

Integrity and loyalty to the king were the benchmarks for rewards in terms of promotion. In order to boost the army's effectiveness, the rulers used to reshuffle it from time to time. Retirement of old soldiers and recruitment of new ones used to take place in addition to promotion and punishment. The legendary historian Baburam Acharya[89] odserved that Jaya Prakash Malla of Kathmandu employed Ranabhim Thapa to counter attack the Gorkhali troops, but when the force of 8000 infantry was about to depart for the campaign, arrested him for conspiracy on the charge of working for the enemy. He then appointed Kashi Ram Thapa as the new army commander. Kashiram Thapa himself was later executed along with eight others on suspicion of conspiracy.[90]

---

86. Baidya, *Ancient and Medieval Military History of Nepal* (ed.), n. 1, p. 19.
87. Nath, Yogi Narahari and Baburam Acharya, *King Prithvi Narayan Shah's Dibya Upadesh,* p. 7.
88. Baidya, *Ancient and Medieval Military History of Nepal* (ed.), n. 1, p. 19.
89. Ibid., p. 21.
90. Ibid.

Dhanbajra Bajracharya,[91] another historian, notes that service in the army was remunerated from the ancient times in land or other lucrative gifts. The names of such beneficiaries were listed in the inscriptions of the Licchavi era as well.[92] In the protocol list of the time, the higher ranks of the military coincided with even the crown prince, based on their experience, service and qualification.[93]

The Malla regimes in the medieval period, being poor, initially employed limited army staff, but later, when the Gorkhali troops encircled Kathmandu Valley, were compelled to increase their numbers. Jaya Prakash Malla recruited 200 Nagarkoti from Kumaon/Garhwal as there was shortage of martial people. To maintain the army, he borrowed from the temple trusts.[94] King Bishnu Malla of Lalitpur also borrowed the jewellery he had donated to the Pasupati Nath temple, promising to return double the amount if he won in the military endeavour.[95]

In the ancient and medieval periods, the rule of law was based on religion, myths and traditions. In this regard, most of the rulers followed in the footsteps of their forefathers. The exceptional cases have been discredited by history, as noted in subsequent paragraphs and chapters. Mostly, it was the military officers who used to run the day-to-day general administration as well. In the absence of a standard law, the measure of reward and punishment varied. For example, Kaji Bhim Malla, who was assigned by King Pratap Malla to launch an operation in Tibet, collected illegal property and wealth there. On return, he betrayed the state and allied with the king of Bhaktapur against King Pratap Malla. The king then had him executed.[96]

Military Strategy

Ancient Hindu tradition describes the state's seven assets to enhance its strength as: king, minister, nation, fort, treasury, army and friends.[97] Almost all the Nepalese rulers followed this doctrine. Regarding the military matters, they realised that numerical strength is not enough but a realistic and practical

91. *"Lichchhabi Kal ko Sasan Paddhati", Purnima*, Issue 25, p. 248.
92. Ibid., pp. 245, 419.
93. Baidya, *Ancient and Medieval Military History of Nepal* (ed.), n. 1, p. 22.
94. Ibid.
95. Lamsal, Pandit Devi Prasad, *Bhasa Bamsabali* (ed.), *Part II*, Kathmandu: Nepal National Library, Archaeological Division, 1968, p. 114.
96. Ibid., p. 74.
97. Baidya, *Ancient and Medieval Military History of Nepal* (ed.), n. 1, p. 25.

strategy is necessary to win battles. The available genealogy and pedigree, records and inscriptions of the medieval period spoke about the strategy that followed. Whenever an aggression took place, the rulers consulted fortune-tellers for the right time to carry out an assault, torch the nearby places or the target itself, encircle the area and apply the policy of *sam, dam, dand, bhed*[98] so that the enemy would surrender.[99] Setting fire was a common tactic. Jitari Malla, his son Aditya[100] as well as the ruler of Simroungarh not only set fire to Kathmandu Valley's dwellings but also destroyed partially the Pashupatinath Temple in 1311.[101] Sultan Shamsuddhin Ilyas, a Muslim ruler of Bengal, torched the Kathmandu Valley in 1349.[102] King Mukunda Sen of Palpa similarly torched places of strategic importance in the Kathmandu Valley in 1525-26.[103]

Encirclement of the enemy troops was another tactic, as elaborated in the *Gopalraj-Bamsawali*.[104] Khas Malla ruler Jitari and Aditya Malla encircled the Kathmandu Valley for almost a month. Prithvi Narayan Shah leaned heavily on diplomacy. He also applied the "outpost technique" to isolate the enemy from outside support.[105] But Prithvi Narayan Shah experienced defeat in Kirtipur in 1757 despite having extensively prepared for war, losing his close ally Kalu Pande. He himself survived because a soldier in Malla's army had an inhibition about killing a monarch.[106]

Two years later, Prithvi Narayan Shah imposed an economic embargo on the Kathmandu Valley, encircling it from all directions, and focused on Kirtipur as his base to launch an offensive. As he had been defeated twice in Kirtipur itself, the town was heavily cordoned by the Gorkhali troops. The Gorkhalis also

---

98. *Sam*: the enemy should be first urged to desist; failing which, *dam* (offering a financial incentive) should be tried; failing which, *dand* (punishment) follows; *bhed* is creating division amongst the enemy's allies to weaken him. Chanakya, Chandra Gupta Maurya's advisor, emphasised this doctrine.

99. Baidya, *Ancient and Medieval Military History of Nepal* (ed.), n. 1, p. 25.

100. Bajracharya, Dhanbajra and Malla, Kamal P., *The Gopalrajbamshi*, Kathmandu: Nepal Research Centre, 1985, p. 89.

101. Ibid., pp. 98-99.

102. Whelpton, *A History of Nepal*, n. 3, p. 21.

103. Pant, Mahesh Raj and Pant, Dinesh Raj, *Nepal Khaldo ma Raja Mukund Sen ko Hamala*, *Purnima*, Issue 45, p. 8.

104. Bajracharya and Malla, *The Gopalrajbamshi*, n. 27, p. 104.

105. Stiller, Ludwig F., *The Rise of the House of Gorkha*, _________: HRD Research Centre, revised edition, 1995, p. 89.

106. Baidya, *Ancient and Medieval Military History of Nepal* (ed.), n. 1, p. 32.

kidnapped a son of Kaji Dhanwant, the warlord responsible for fighting for the Malla rulers of the Kathmandu Valley, and took him to Nuwakot to bargain with the father. Prithvi Narayan Shah also slashed the noses and ears of any of the youths who resisted his conquest of the Kathmandu Valley.[107]

In earlier times, the Kathmandu Valley dwellers avoided battle against invaders like Khas Malla of Western Nepal and Shamsuddhin Ilyas of Bengal. The regime as well as the elites hid away their property and food grains and themselves hid in the nearby forest or in forts, from where they fought guerrilla warfare.[108] These forts still exist in places like Swayambhu Chaityagadh, Balaju, Gokarna, Chagu, Bajrayogini, Farping, etc.

Jitari Malla invaded the Kathmandu Valley in 1288, but the Kathmandu Valley dwellers, applying guerrilla tactics, in a single night killed 800 soldiers. When Shamsuddhin Ilyas invaded the valley in 1350, the Kathmandu Valley dwellers escaped from their houses for seven days. The invading forces torched all the empty houses. But due to the approaching cold and the guerrilla techniques used by the defenders, Shamsuddhin's forces withdrew.[109] Earlier, three major aggressions were repulsed by the Kathmandu Malla rulers, namely, the aggressions of the rulers of Simroungarh, Shamsuddhin Ilyas of Bengal, and Mukunda Sen of Palpa.

Deception was also used to trap the enemy. When, with the support of Baisi and Chaubisi estate, Lumjung captured the strategically located Liglig Kot from the Gorkha state, Gorkhali ruler Prithvi Pati Shah's son Ranadal suggested to his father to make pretence of disinheriting and disowning him, forcing the son to take shelter in Lamjung's state. Ranadal not only got shelter with Lumjung but also took command of Liglig Kot itself. At an opportune time, he informed his father to launch a counter offensive to recapture Liglig Kot.[110]

Prithvi Narayan Shah was one of Nepal's greatest strategists. When he repeatedly failed to conquer the Kathmandu Valley and surrounding states, he studied the war history of previous invaders and decided to employ deception to weaken his adversaries. He used the ancient tactic of *bhed* (creating division amongst the enemy's allies to weaken him): he caused division among the Malla royal families, rift among the three Malla rulers of the Kathmandu Valley, created

107. Ibid.
108. Ibid., pp. 32-33.
109. Bajracharya and Malla, *The Gopalrajbamshi,* n. 27, p. 34.
110. Hasrat, Bikramjit, *History of Nepal*, Hosiyarpur: V.V. Research Institute, 1970, p. 123.

mistrust between the king and the court, and used propaganda and rumours to subvert the people against the regime and align with the enemy.[111]

Both offensive and defensive weapons were used both in conventional warfare as well as to quell insurgencies. Offensive weapons consisted of sword, dagger and knife, axe and lance; defensive weapons comprised shield, armour plate and helmet. Later on, the invention of gunpowder enabled the use of guns and cannon. The military philosophy of the Nepali rulers mainly comprised offensive tactics, with defence being secondary.

Malla rulers had a good inventory of guns and cannon. Prithvi Narayan Shah also gathered a few guns from Banaras City in India. After his victory in the Kathmandu Valley, he confiscated the guns in the area.[112] Baisi and Chaubisi, Palpa as well as Lamjung also had many guns. In the process of integrating greater Nepal, Prince Bahadur Shah (Prithvi Narayan Shah's son) confiscated all these weapons.

The Gorkha made their own cannon. The one that Prince Chandra Rup Shah fabricated in 1714 is still on show at the Rang Mahal of Gorkha Palace.[113] Gorkhali troops also captured more than 500 guns from the invading forces of Mir Kassim in 1763 and later, 300 guns and some cannon from the invading British East India Company under Captain Kinlochin in the Battle of Pauwagadi in 1767. Those captured weapons were used by the Gorkhali troops in the expansion campaign of greater Nepal. As their military ambitions grew, the Gorkhalis' strategy also refined step-by-step.

In the ancient and medieval eras, the Licchavi rulers had basically applied religious myth and faith to run the affairs of state including the military. The stone inscriptions of those eras do not indicate concrete military strategy in particular.[114] But rulers like Narendra Dev were much influenced by the Maurya dynasty in India vis-à-vis China. Narendra Dev supported a huge number of cavalry and infantry. This can be explained by Kautilya's political economy and Sun-Tzu's theory of war. Prithvi Narayan Shah envisioned in his *Dibya Upadesh* that imperial China in the north and the British in the south were crucial powers to be balanced for Nepal's survival.

111. The technique was further elaborated by Kautilya.
112. Baidya, Tulsi Ram, *Prithvi Narayan Shah– Ranajit Mallakalin Kagaj Patra,* Kathmandu: Nepal Research Institute, 1971.
113. Baidya, Bajracharya, *Gorkha ko Aitihasik Samagri,* Kathmandu: Nepal Research Institute, 1972, p. 19.
114. Baidya, *Ancient and Medieval Military History of Nepal* (ed.), n. 1, p. 35.

Integration of Modern Nepal

The 1700s was a century of colonialism by the Western powers. Britain, France and Portugal consolidated power in the South and South East Asia. The feuding principalities of Nepal were not serious about the British move in the South, but the visionary king of the principality of Gorkha determined to unify Nepal to counter the British invasion. The unification campaign was initiated in CE 1740 at the same time that the British were consolidating power in India. After capturing Kathmandu Valley in 1743, the Gorkhali armed forces were known as the Nepali Army.[115]

The Gorkha military starts its history from the time of Drabya Shah, who founded the Gorkha kingdom. The neighbouring Lamjung, Tanahu and Kaski states were its rivals and frequent skirmishes took place with them. Gorkha was poor economically. It had almost no trade with Tibet although it shared a border with that country. Its main source of income was agriculture and animal husbandry. Kings like Ram Shah tried to explore trade with the Kathmandu Valley. Prithvi Pati Shah involved the Gorkha in his kingdom's politics. Nara Bhupal Shah wanted to expand his territory but failed in invading Nuwakot. With this failure, Prithvi Narayan Shah realised the importance of strengthening the military.[116]

In the 16th and 17th centuries, Tibet was weak because of the struggle of the Buddhist sects of Lhasa and Shigatse.[117] Ram Shah of Gorkha (1606-33) and Pratap Malla of Kathmandu (1624-74) seized this opportunity to control the border pass through which most of the trans-Himalayan trade was carried out. In their second attempt, the Gorkhali defeated the Tibetans at Khinchog and advanced into Kerong. Ultimately, Tibet and Gorkha reached an agreement to draw their boundary at Kukurghat, enabling Ram Shah to control the main communication line between Nepal and Tibet.[118]

Prithvi Narayan Shah - Founder of Modern Nepal

With the legacy of Ram Shah, Prithvi Pati Shah and Nara Bhupal Shah, Prithvi Narayan Shah was sworn to the crown in his early 20s. He had the dream of

115. http://nepalarmy.mil.np/history.php?
116. Bajracharya, Bhadra Ratna, *Sainik Sangathan Ra Prasasan* (ed.), in *Military History of Nepal (Part I)*, Royal Nepal Army Headquarters, 1992, p. 76.
117. Rose, *Nepal: Strategy for Survival*, n. 6, p. 13.
118. Ibid.

expanding Gorkha as a bigger and powerful state. He wanted to conquer the Kathmandu Valley but feared that the Western states might attack his kingdom in his absence. He sought the advice of Crown Prince Uddhot Sen of Palpa in this regard:

> *'Uncle!! I have been to Makwanpur. I saw Nepal too. I have a strong intention to capture it. Please advise me.' To answer him, Uddhot Sen compared Lamjung to an eagle, Gorkha to a snake and Kathmandu Valley to a frog. If the snake wants to swallow the frog, it has to be safe from the eagle.*[119]

Heeding this advice, Prithvi Narayan Shah went on to build a strong and credible military. He also concluded a treaty with the Gorkha's long-time rival Lamjung at Chepeghat, an alliance facilitated by his trusted ally Kalu Pande.[120] The friendship with Lamjung helped Prithvi Narayan Shah to secure Gorkha from Baisi and Chaubisi states of the West.

As the military expanded, King Prithvi Narayan Shah needed to generate income. The Malla rulers had a good partnership with the Kashmiri traders from Banaras and Gosain (Hindu merchant-pilgrims), whom he suspected to be spying for the East India Company and expelled them.[121] He advocated economic self-sufficiency and trade by local rather than Indian merchants. During his campaign against the Valley states, he hampered the British attempts to establish trading relations and access to Tibet.[122]

Box 2.1. Nepal's first regimental units

> Prithvi Narayan Shah formed four companies, namely Sri Nath, Kalibox, Barda Bahadur, and Sabuj initially, and Purano Gorakh later, with the weapons seized by Mir Kasim – an invader in 1763. It was the first rank and file system beginning the modern organisational history of Nepali Army.

Source: History of the Nepalese Army, http:/nepalarmy.mi.np/history.php?page=two

As a result, Gorkha revenue declined. To meet the contingency and to control unwanted immigrants, King Prithvi Narayan Shah established a trade mart in Parsa Gari, en route to India, and at several points on the Tibetan border. He insisted on trade by the Nepali merchants, which was not acceptable to Tibet.

119. Bajracharya, *Sainik Sangathan Ra Prasasan* (ed.), n. 43, p. 77.
120. Ibid., p. 78.
121. Rose, *Nepal: Strategy for Survival*, n. 6, p. 25.
122. Whelpton, *A History of Nepal*, n. 3, p. 39.

Consequently, Tibet closed the trade marts on its border in 1770 and suspended all commercial dealings with Nepal.[123]

To counter King Prithvi Narayan Shah's nascent ambition of nationhood, the British turned to Bhutan to meet their trading demands with Tibet. Deb Raj Desi Shidariva, a temporal authority in Bhutan, seized the Chumbi valley in 1768-69, then part of Sikkim, and controlled the major routes to Tibet. He also captured Cooch Bihar but had to return it in 1772 after the British intervention. In order to seize trade routes, King Prithvi Narayan Shah launched a campaign towards Eastern Nepal. He captured Morang in Tarai and the adjoining Northern Olang Chung Gola pass to control the Tibetan route as well as the British avenues in the South.[124]

While he was consolidating power internally, the Tibetans objected to the supply of low-quality coins minted in Nepal. Jaya Prakash Malla and Ranajit Malla, the rulers of Kathmandu and Bhaktapur respectively, had mixed lower-quality metals with silver to mint the coins, to be able to meet the growing expenditure incurred in the war with Gorkhali. When King Prithvi Narayan Shah took over, he did not concede to the Tibetan demand.[125]

King Prithvi Narayan Shah visualised Nepal as being a yam between two boulders, namely, the emperor of the South (India) who was much too clever, and the sleeping giant in the North (China), whom it was prudent not to wake up.[126] His vision is still relevant for Nepal's foreign policy outlook. King Prithvi Narayan Shah geared up integrating Nepal once he conquered the Kathmandu Valley with the help of the Nepali Army from 1744.

After King Prithvi Narayan Shah's demise at the age of 51 in 1775, the process of Nepal's unification was taken up by his successors. But the process remained fragmented due to palace conspiracy, plagued by inequalities in terms of class, gender, ethnicity, language, culture and religion.[127] This was a betrayal of King Prithvi Narayan Shah's philosophy on national integration, which was based on the premise that Nepal was a common garden of flowers (in other words, people) irrespective of caste, class, tribe or religion.

---

123. Rose, *Nepal: Strategy for Survival*, n. 6, p. 25.
124. Ibid., p. 27.
125. *History of the Nepalese Army*, http://nepalarmy.mil.np/history.php?page=three
126. Bhattarai, Umesh K., *Conflict to Peace: Transition in Nepal,* New Delhi: Adarsh Books, 2014, p. 16.
127. Ibid.

However, Prithvi Narayan Shah was blamed by historians for his statement that Nepal was the "*real* Hindustan", which might have hurt non-Hindus in Nepal.[128] Thus, he failed to become inclusive to unite the country in the creation of a nation-state as such. But according to Tri-Ratna Manandhar,[129] cultural integration has no linkage with the working of an army. So, the Nepal Army should have worked on the principle of unity in diversity, as per his vision expressed in *Dibya Upadesh.*

In order to integrate Nepal, King Prithvi Narayan Shah showed a high level of strategic vision in balancing relations with Tibet, Bhutan, Sikkim, the East India Company and China. Tibet was crucial from the trading point of view. After the victory of Nuwakot, his first step was to control the transit points like Kerung and Kuti pass to encircle the Kathmandu Valley. He successfully gained virtual monopoly on trade between the Southern plain of India and the Northern plateau of Tibet. In the critical period of 1769-88 (Prithvi Narayan Shah died in 1775), the Kathmandu court had to constantly struggle to open alternative routes through military campaigning in the hill areas East and West of Kathmandu from where to fulfil its economic objectives.[130]

Violence in the process of integrating a nation is inevitable. Both King Prithvi Narayan Shah and his successors used coercive tactics to attain their objective. When King Prithvi Narayan Shah encountered resistance by some youths of Kirtipur (a hillock adjoining Kantipur) when he was preparing for the final assault on the Kathmandu Valley, he had their ears and noses slashed, despite his promise that he would not kill the villagers in the process.[131] But the people of Kirtipur still remember this incident as an insult to the natives by an invader. The Nepali history has also evidence of a formal order issued by then Regent Bahadur Shah (on behalf of the then King Rana Bahadur Shah) to Commander Bhakti Thapa to kill all male youths of Jumla aged 12 years and older who resisted the Nepal Army's drive to annex it into modern Nepal.[132]

Violence and the rewards system were used as tools to achieve political

128. Rawal, Ram Bahadur, *"Rastrabad* vs *Rastraghat"*, Kathmandu: *Nepal Weekly*, 13 November 2011, pp.17-18.
129. Professor Manandhar, former Vice-Chancellor of Lumbini Buddhist University of Nepal, in an interview with the author on 2 October 2016.
130. Rose, *Nepal: Strategy for Survival*, n. 6, p. 25.
131. Acharya, Baburam, *Nepal ko Samchhipta Britant,* Kathmandu: Prof Krishna Prasad Acharya, 1970, p. 148.
132. Pant, Mahesh Raj, *Bir Bhakti Thapa*, *Purnima Anka* 10, 1966, pp. 41-42.

and strategic objectives. Land was distributed to the favoured ones under the Birta and jagir systems.[133] John Whelpton, a Hong Kong-based historian and linguist, comments that King Prithvi Narayan Shah's success rested partly on sound logistical preparations but even more on his political skills and a shrewd combination of conciliation and intimidation.[134]

In the rise of the Gorkha, however, the final assimilation of the occupied territory was undertaken by the Gorkhali commanders. In the series of bitter engagements that culminated in Gorkhali victory over the Raja of Sikkim at Eastern Chainpur in 1776, the Limbus in the Gorkhali army were used. These were the first of many recruits from among the people of occupied territories. Their recruitment established a standard pattern in the ensuing years. Recruiting men of the fighting caste throughout Greater Nepal made both the growth of the Gorkhali Army and the unification of Nepal possible.[135] Perhaps inspired by this vision, David Ochterlony and the British Political Agent William Fraser quickly decided to enrol the Gorkhali in the British Army in 1815 during the Anglo-Nepal War of 1814-16.

Nepal's Integration in Regency Period

The military remained the focal point for Nepal's legendary leaders like Bahadur Shah, the Regent Queen Rajendra Laxmi and Bhimsen Thapa, who continued the expansion campaign of King Prithvi Narayan Shah. Nepal's boundary reached the Sutlej in the West and the Tista in the East, but the campaign was stymied by the British, who forced Nepal to sign the Sughauli Treaty in 1816, confining Nepal to its present boundary. Palace intrigue was the main cause of this development: Bahadur Shah was executed and Bhimshen Thapa committed suicide in custody. Historians claim that Bhimsen Thapa ruled the country through his own philosophy of democracy with the help of 6000 core military groups terrorising the opponents.[136]

Under Bahadur Shah and Bhimsen Thapa, the Nepalis annexed not only the hill states of the Gandaki and Karnali basin but also Kumaon and Garhwal,

133. Basnett, Yurendra, *From Politicization of Grievances to Political Violence: An Analysis of the Maoist Movement in Nepal*, _________: __________, 2009.
134. Whelpton, *A History of Nepal*, n. 3, p. 3.
135. Stiller, *The Rise of the House of Gorkha*, n. 32, p.126.
136. Dhungel, Ramesh, "*Swadhinta Ra Desh Bhakti Ko Apabakhya*", *Kantipur Daily*, ________ 2010, p. 6.

which are now part of the Indian state of Uttarakhand.[137] The westward drive was halted partially due to Nepal's aggressive policy towards Tibet over trade and border issues, triggering a Chinese invasion.[138] Also, Ranjit Singh, the ruler of Punjab, checked Nepal's westward annexation on the Sutlej in the winter of 1809-10.[139]

Bahadur Shah – An Able Son of Nepal

Bahadur Shah successfully campaigned to expand the westward territory of Baisi and Chaubisi, including Kumaon and Garhwal, which his father King Prithvi Narayan Shah failed to annex.[140] When Kathmandu was conquered, he was 13-years-old. King Prithvi Narayan Shah ruled most of the time from Nuwakot rather than the capital Kathmandu, which was left in the charge of his eldest son Pratap Singh Shah.[141] Bahadur Shah inherited from his father qualities of leadership and aggressiveness. He was also well-acquainted with the Gorkhali military customs.[142]

The Nepali court was divided on who should succeed King Prithvi Narayan Shah as the king. Although the father was well-informed about Pratap Singh Shah's weaknesses and most of the courtiers disliked him, he chose him as his successor, prioritising seniority and tradition.[143] After King Prithvi Narayan Shah's death in 1775, Pratap Singh Shah ascended the throne. He initially imprisoned Bahadur Shah and later exiled him to Tanahu first and then to Bettiah (currently in the state of Bihar in India).

Upon Pratap Singh Shah's death in 1777, Bahadur Shah was called by the Nepali court to assist the state. The queen mother Rajendra Laxmi and Bahadur Shah then became Nepal's joint regents. Bahadur Shah was assigned foreign affairs, but he was not happy with the queen's working style, because she was reluctant to expand Nepal as envisioned by his father. Some courtiers told Rajendra Laxmi that if he was given an opportunity to go for a military campaign, he might capture power. She then imprisoned him.[144]

137. Whelpton, *A History of Nepal*, n. 3, p. 39.
138. Ibid.
139. Ibid., p. 42.
140. Ibid., p. 39.
141. Bajrachayra, B.R., *Bahadur Shah: The Regent of Nepal*, Delhi: Anmol, 1992, pp. 2-3.
142. Stiller, *The Rise of the House of Gorkha*, n. 32, p. 148.
143. Ibid.
144. Ibid.

Meanwhile, Rajendra Laxmi was accused by most of the courtiers of misusing state revenues for a private luxurious life and sexual misconduct with her close ally. She was then arrested by Bahadur Shah's faction led by Daljit Shah, the Chief Chautaria (first minister) in her regency.[145] In this chronology, almost three years passed without any accomplishment for the consolidation of Nepal after King Prithvi Narayan Shah's death. The Nepal court supported Bahadur Shah unanimously and he became sole regent for the infant King Rana Bahadur Shah.

But soon, the tide of events turned against Bahadur Shah. He arrested his mother and had her alleged paramour killed. She was in custody for ten months and then was found not guilty. Meanwhile, Bahadur Shah, who had no practical knowledge of warfare, failed in invading Chaubisi, a strong state in the West.[146] Due to a coalition of Chaubisi with Palpa, the Nepali Army had to retreat from Tanahu in 1779. This retreat turned the tide against Bahadur Shah and the regent queen was again declared regent. Bahadur Shah was then sent in exile to Bettiah.

Box 2.2. Regiments formed during Regent Queen Rajendra Laxmi's regime (1779-84)

Sri Meher-1, Sri Meher-2, Bhawani Box, Naya Gorakh, Srijung, Ranabhim, Jwala Dal, Tara Dal, Bhairabi Dal, Batuk Dal, Durga Box, Kali Dal, Devi Dutta, Sri Nath, Ram Dal, Raj Dal, Barakh.

Source: Military History of Nepal Part 1, 1992, p. 103.

Rajendra Laxmi was aware of Bahadur Shah's administrative competency and was chary of being overshadowed by him. Encouraged by this family dispute, Chaubisi were organising a counter offensive against Gorkha and contacted the East India Company for weapons and other materials. After getting this information, the queen regent contacted Bahadur Shah, asking him to exercise his influence to convince the Company government not to accede to their demands.

After the regent queen died in 1785, Bahadur Shah became the sole regent for nine years. On his return to power, he generated a new spirit in the military activity. He recalled the people who had been exiled for hatching a conspiracy against the queen regent and even during the time of Pratap Singh Shah. He appointed capable officers with jagirs in the army. It took almost a year for

145. Ibid., p. 21.
146. Ibid., p. 25.

Bahadur Shah to purge the army.[147] His regency period is considered the golden age of Nepal's unification.[148] The first comprehensive scrutiny of the army's rank-and-file took place under his command.

However, Bahadur Shah was an oppressive ruler in contrast to his father.[149] King Prithvi Narayan Shah always apprehended resistance from the Chaubisi while he was expanding eastward, but had an easy mind while he was expanding westward. Some historians believe that he bribed the Chaubisi to not invade Gorkha while he was engaged in the east. Bahadur Shah on the other hand neither played a defensive role nor realised that such policy was essential because his eastern flank was always secured.[150]

One of the lessons Bahadur Shah had learned from his father was: "Win over the enemy or factions of the enemy. Be generous to those who cooperate with you; harsh with those who oppose you."[151] He consistently bribed those who submitted to Gorkhali rule. He overran the west, including Chaubisi and a large area of Tarai in a very short span of time, which he dispensed as jagirs to hill men who opted to join the army.[152] His war strategy was mainly influenced by the strengthened position of Gorkha during his regime.[153]

Because Bahadur Shah was ruthless in his dealings, his opponents acted as fifth columnists wherever they found weaknesses among the invading Gorkhalis. At many places in the West, when news about the arrival of Gorkhalis came, the locals left their homesteads.[154] But Bahadur Shah dealt benignly with those who surrendered. He had a policy of dependent states, on which he differed from his father.

Box 2.3. Regiments formed in Regent Bahadur Shah's regime

Kali Dal, Bhawani Dal, Ranashardul, Gurubox, Bhairab, Ranasur, Ajaya Dal, Singhnath, Ranasher, Ranabam, Jabarjung, Hanumandhoj, Gorakhbox, Gauribox, Siddhibox, Sribox, Ranabom, Bir-chandra jung, Rana Dal, Sri Dal, Sri Bhagwati Dal—formed between 1785-1793.

Source: Military History of Nepal, Part 1, 1992, p. 104.

147. Ibid., p. 36.
148. Ibid., p. 148.
149. Bajracharya, *Sainik Sangathan Ra Prasasan* (ed.), n. 43, p. 62.
150. Ibid.
151. Stiller, *The Rise of the House of Gorkha*, n. 32, p. 153.
152. Ibid., p. 154.
153. Bajracharya, *Sainik Sangathan Ra Prasasan* (ed.), n. 43, p. 62.
154. Ibid.

Bahadur Shah's westward expansion campaign was fully successful but the war with Tibet and China's involvement in it weakened his effort. His westward movement was disrupted due to continued clash with Tibet over minting of impure silver coins[155] and Nepal's decision to give refuge to Syamarpa Lama, who fled Tibet on religious and political grounds with his 14 Tibetan followers.[156] Another contentious issue was the low quality salt Tibet was supplying to Nepal.[157] Tibet not only ignored this issue but also decided to close trade routes.[158] Tibet also encouraged the principalities of Jumla in Western Nepal to renew their sporadic hostilities with Gorkhalis.[159] Jumla immediately seized Mustang and surroundings. (Gorkhalis recaptured it immediately after their stalemate with Tibet was over.)[160]

It is possible that Bahadur Shah had made a mistake in opening up a two-front war.[161] His father always believed in a single-front war. The westward expansion campaign was ongoing when he decided to fight with Tibet. Although he succeeded, concluding with a treaty with Tibet in 1789, Tibet's resentment led China to get involved in a war with Nepal in 1792.

The Nepal-Tibet War of 1788 concluded with a treaty the following year, which ceded annual grants to Nepal in the border areas.[162] Prior to the war, Tibet first sought military support of the British from General Charles Cornwallis. But he declined to send an army to Sigatse, citing three reasons: (i) it would be too expensive a campaign; (ii) the Company had not suffered any provocation or injury from the Gorkha kingdom; and (iii) the Chinese Emperor might be displeased.[163] Bahadur Shah then concluded a trade treaty with the British in 1791, despite continuing misgivings among his courtiers, in the hope that it would help in case of a war with China.[164] But the British declined his repeated appeals for purchase of weapons and ammunition, because Tibet also was looking out for weapons from them.[165] They instead sent Colonel William Kirkpatrick

155. Stiller, *The Rise of the House of Gorkha*, n. 32, p. 161.
156. *History of Nepalese Army*, http://nepalarmy.mil.np/history.php?
157. Ibid.
158. Rose, *Nepal: Strategy for Survival*, n. 6, p. 37.
159. Ibid., p. 40.
160. Ibid.
161. Acharya, *Nepal ko Samchhipta Britant,* n. 58, p. 254.
162. Ibid., p. 42.
163. Ibid., p. 40.
164. Whelpton, *A History of Nepal,* n. 3, p. 39.
165. Acharya, *Nepal ko Samchhipta Britant,* n. 58, p. 254.

as envoy to Kathmandu in 1793, some months after the Chinese withdrawal.[166] Kirkpatrick's presence was a political embarrassment for Bahadur Shah for his association with the British. Hence, he was recalled after some time.

Box 2.4: Summary of Nepal-Tibet Treaty, 1789

1.	Nepal agreed to withdraw from four border districts of Tibet occupied during the hostilities.
2.	Tibet agreed to pay annual tribute of 300 *dotsed* of silver.
3.	Tibet agreed to accept and use the newly minted Nepali coins.
4.	Nepal promised never to invade Tibet again.
5.	Nepal was granted the right to maintain an envoy in Lhasa.
6.	Trade between Tibet and India was to be channelled solely through Nepal, and the alternative trade routes through Sikkim and Bhutan were to be closed.
7.	A Tibetan lama was to visit Kathmandu each year "to bless the temple, i.e., Swayambhu Nath".

Source: Leo E. Rose, Nepal: Struggle for Survival, pp. 42-43.

The Chinese then questioned the legitimacy of the 1979 Nepal-Tibet treaty. Nepal had demanded full compensation for war expenses and "50 *dharnis* of gold" which, under the 1775 treaty was to be paid by the government that violated the agreement. No single authoritative text of this treaty was available, except for only a number of letters exchanged between the contracting authorities.[167] The issue became quite controversial as Chinese officials were invited to witness after the treaty had already been signed.

For Bahadur Shah it became a matter of prestige to prove the legitimacy of the treaty because the young king Rana Bahadur Shah was approaching an age of understanding the affairs of state. Bahadur Shah had also to manage the misinformation fed to the future king by his critics. It was imperative for him to convince the Nepali durbar to continue the Tibet operation on the ground that Tibet failed to fulfil the agreements of the 1789 treaty. As a result, 4,000 Nepali troops again invaded the Tibet border on 6 August 1791.[168]

China had reservations over the process in which the 1789 treaty was concluded. The Chinese emperor instructed the Governor of Szechuan, who was responsible to look after Tibet affairs, to warn the Nepali leaders that a Chinese army would be sent to Tibet and that Nepal would be treated much

166. Whelpton, *A History of Nepal,* n. 3, p. 39.
167. Rose, *Nepal: Strategy for Survival,* n. 6, pp. 41-42.
168. Ibid., p. 52.

more severely than in 1789.[169] China got involved in the Nepal-Tibet War in 1791-93. Upon the end of the war, the two sides agreed on various terms, which remain a foundation pillar of their bilateral relations even today.

Box 2.5: Agreement on the conclusion of Nepal-China War, 1792

1. Nepal and Tibet will maintain fraternal relations and will not engage in mutual hostilities.
2. Nepal will send a mission to Peking every five years with a gift for the emperor. The Chinese government will arrange facilities for the mission in China (i.e., bear the cost involved) and will send a gift to the Nepali Raja in return.
3. A Chinese officer will demarcate the boundary between Nepal and Tibet in the Kuti and Kerong area.
4. China will come to Nepal's assistance in the event of an attack by a foreign power.
5. Nepal will return the articles seized at Tashilhunpo monastery.
6. Nepal will never again raise claims based on the 1789 treaty or the coinage question.

Source: Leo E. Rose, Nepal: Strategy for Survival, p. 65.

Tibet was China's protectorate from 1720 onwards. The meddling of the ambitious ruling lamas invited this state of affairs. Samarpa Lama, for example, wanted to gain the wealth of his deceased brother Panchen Lama, who had gone to Peking to congratulate the Emperor on the occasion of his 70th anniversary, and passed away there. Another of Panchen Lama's brothers, Chung-pa Hutukhtu, captured all the property. Consequently, Samarpa Lama fled from the Tashilunpo monastery to Kathmandu in 1781 and complained to the Nepali Durbar.[170] This induced the durbar to invade Tibet. King Prithvi Narayan Shah believed in a non-threatening relationship with China as well as the British. Bahadur Shah changed this policy approach.[171]

De Facto Power in Regency Period

Rana Bahadur Shah allowed himself to be manipulated by his childhood friend Bhimsen Thapa. The latter, though he was not the regent, exercised de facto rule after Rana Bahadur Shah's death. Rana Bahadur Shah named himself Mukhtiyar[172] of his son King Girban Yuddha Bikram Shah. After the Nepal-China War of 1792, in the annual Pajani (annual reinvestment in office)

169. Ibid., p. 53.
170. Stiller, *The Rise of the House of Gorkha*, n. 32, p. 163.
171. Rose, *Nepal: Strategy for Survival*, n. 6, p. 65.
172. A post equivalent to Prime Minister with full executive powers.

ceremony in July 1792,[173] Bahadur Shah was not reappointed as Chautaria (first minister).

Rana Bahadur Shah - a De-facto to Griban Yuddha

Rana Bahadur then assumed full king's powers in 1794. He ordered Bahadur Shah to leave the palace in favour of his nephews.[174] Chautaria Bidhur Shahi and Sher Bahadur Shahi (the king's stepbrothers) then occupied the palace.[175] Rana Bahadur was angry because Bahadur Shah had requested the Amban (the Chinese emperor's representative in Lhasa) to forward a letter to the emperor. Rana Bahadur Shah came to know of this from the Amban,[176] which he may have taken as his endeavour to invoke Chinese intervention in Nepal's internal politics.

In reply to Bahadur Shah, the Amban simply suggested reconciliation and sent a copy of the letter to Rana Bahadur as well.[177] But Bahadur Shah insisted on visiting Peking to meet the emperor. The Amban wanted the king's consent for this, which Rana Bahadur declined.[178] The king then imprisoned Bahadur Shah and the latter died in custody in 1797. Some historians are of the view that Rana Bahadur Shah wanted him to accept the charges made against him, which Bahadur Shah rejected, and hence was murdered.[179] It is suspected that Bahadur Shah plotted to depose Rana Bahadur and place his half-brother Sher Bahadur Shah on the throne.[180] For China on the other hand Nepal was of value as a buffer against confrontation with the British.[181] Leo E. Rose in his *Nepal: Strategy for Survival,* quotes Francis Buchanan-Hamilton, who wrote *An Account of the Kingdom of Nepal* in 1819, as follows:

> *The Gorkhalis are in the habit of saying, that, should they have any dispute with the English, their only formidable neighbour, they will claim the protection of the Chinese, with whose influence over the Company they seem to be much better acquainted than one would have expected.*

173. Rose, *Nepal: Strategy for Survival,* n. 6, p. 72.
174. Nepal, Gyanmani, *Nepal ko Mahabharat,* ______: Sajha Prakasan, 1993, p. 36.
175. Acharya, *Nepal ko Samchhipta Britant,* n. 60, p. 257.
176. Rose, *Nepal: Strategy for Survival,* n. 6, p. 72.
177. Ibid.
178. Acharya, *Nepal ko Samchhipta Britant,* n. 60, p. 258.
179. Op. cit., Nepal. p. 40
180. Rose, *Nepal: Strategy for Survival,* n. 6, p. 72.
181. Ibid. p. 73.

Stiller says that overall, the Gorkhali did not want a war. If they continued fighting, their westward movement could have been hampered.[182] The Chinese occupying south of the Himalayas would also have invited direct confrontation with the British. In any case, they were not deprived of their sovereignty. Some argue that the Gorkhali had to pay tribute to the Chinese, but Stiller points out that there is no evidence of this.[183]

By the Trade Treaty of 1791, the British had promised Bahadur Shah to help Nepal in case of any external aggression but failed in their promise when later on China attacked Nepal. Subsequently, China and Nepal signed an agreement on the conclusion of the war in 1792. The British were also requested by Tibet for support before the Chinese intervention in the war. When they failed to accede to the request, they lost the Tibetan market and also earned the suspicion of the Gorkhalis.[184] Leo E. Rose noted how Kathmandu lost the game in its effort at balancing China against the British. The British had by then comprehended the Chinese interest in south of the Himalayas, which became a major consideration for their policy towards Nepal and other hill areas in the ensuing period.[185]

In 1839-42, Britain used India as a launching pad to assault the Chinese market to be able to sell the opium produced in India in Chinese territory. The war led to the signing of the Nanjing Treaty in 1842, by which China ceded Hong Kong island to Britain.[186] As a result, Chinese control over Tibet also gradually declined, which became extremely weak after the 1911 Chinese revolution.[187] Although Britain acknowledged Chinese sovereignty over Tibet, it signed a treaty with Tibet in 1914 at Simla that drew an official border line that London wanted. The Chinese were invited to sign, but declined.[188]

For the Nepalese kingdom, being a buffer between Tibet and British India was a matter of concern. But there were no visionary leaders like Prithvi Narayan Shah and Bahadur Shah who would have led a force to influence Tibet, China and Britain along with powerful Maratha and Punjab, who were the other credible forces on par with the Nepali Army.

182. Stiller, *The Rise of the House of Gorkha*, n. 32, p. 175.
183. Ibid.
184. Ibid.
185. Rose, *Nepal: Strategy for Survival*, n. 6, p. 74.
186. Rachman, Gideon, *Easternisation*. London: The Bodley Head, 2016, p. 25.
187. Riedel, Bruce, *JFK's Forgotten Crisis,* New Delhi: HarperCollins, 2016, p. 21.
188. Ibid.

Because of King Prithvi Narayan Shah's determination not to let the British expand northwards through Nepal, they were compelled to pressurise Bhutan, Sikkim and the adjoining states like Cooch Bihar. For this, they wanted their Resident to be placed in Nepal. In the meantime, Rana Bahadur left the throne in order to embrace the monastic life. Later, he went on a pilgrimage to Banaras. Throughout his lifetime, Bhimsen Thapa was his companion.[189]

To increase their influence in Nepal, the British proposed their residency in Nepal in return for a guarantee to confine Rana Bahadur Shah and his team to Banaras.[190] This suited the Nepali court, who were fed up with his atrocious conduct and wanted him to remain outside. The regent queen, Subarna Prabha, decided to accept the offer. The agreement was signed in Patna on 10 April 1802 and Captain Knox arrived Kathmandu on 18 April to become the first residential representative in Kathmandu.[191]

The British were eager to trade with Tibet. Also, since Tibet was a protectorate state of China from 1720, they wanted to disengage it from China to contact Central Asia and ultimately Eastern Europe. Warren Hastings, the first Governor General of East India Company, also hoped that Tibet could serve as a channel of communication with the Chinese court at Peking.[192] In nine months' time, Captain Knox came to know that China had no political influence at all in Nepal's palace. Also, Bhimsen Thapa and his team were instigating Rana Bahadur Shah to lobby against his forced confinement.[193] As part of a grand design, they spread a rumour that Kathmandu was infected with a cholera outbreak and advised the residency to shift to Makawanpur. Meanwhile, the British were engaged in fighting with the Marathas to establish themselves in southwest India. Succeeding in this endeavour, they established a position in Delhi and decided to recall their residency from Kathmandu.[194]

Bhimsen Thapa had successfully projected the notion that Rana Bahadur and himself had the full support of the East India Company[195] and that they

189. Acharya, Baburam, *General Bhimsen Thapa: Yin Lai Maile Jasto Dekhe,* _________: Srikrishna Acharya, 2008.
190. Ibid., p. 9.
191. Ibid.
192. Rose, *Nepal: Strategy for Survival,* n. 6, p. 28.
193. Ibid., p. 11.
194. Ibid., p. 13.
195. Ibid., p. 77.

would not do anything to harm the nation.[196] After their return to Nepal, Bhimsen Thapa rose to power after Rana Bahadur Shah's assassination by his stepbrother Sher Bahadur Shah in the court at midnight. The court had been called by Mukhtiyar Rana Bahadur to investigate corruption charges against Tribhuvan Pradhan, who was the maternal uncle of Sher Bahadur Shah.[197]

Bhimsen Thapa as De-facto Ruler

Bhimsen Thapa was already a "Chautaria"[198] in rank. The junior queen Lalit Tripura-Sundari was his relative. The heir to the throne, Girban Yuddha Bikram Shah, was a minor. Lalit Tripura-Sundari was, under Bhimsen Thapa's grand design, expected to marry Rana Bahadur Shah. Some historians say that Rana Bahadur Shah's assassination was masterminded by Bhimsen Thapa.[199] Once he became the Mukhtiyar, he killed 93 persons, including several of Rana Bahadur's wives, whom he burned on their husband's pyre to ensure that the regency went to the junior queen.[200] His rivals' cremation was done in an insulting manner.[201]

The rise and fall of Bhimsen Thapa typifies Nepal's history of conspiracy, violence and bloodshed. He provoked the corruption case in front of Rana Bahadur Shah and at the climax, vanished from the scene.[202] Ostensibly, he went out with Rana Bahadur's permission to have dinner. Bhimsen Thapa remained in power for 31 years as a prime minster, a commander-in-chief and a mukhtiyar.

After the regent queen Tripura-Sundari's death in 1832, King Rajendra Bikram Shah ousted him. Shortly after, one of the princes died, and Bhimsen Thapa was arrested on the trumped-up charge of poisoning him.[203] Thapa committed suicide in 1839, just the way he used to force his opponents to do,[204] after his rivals told him that his wife would be paraded naked through the streets.[205]

---

196. Acharya, *General Bhimsen Thapa ...*, n. 116, p. 15.
197. Nepal, Gyanmani, *Nepal ko Mahabharat*, n. 101, p. 70.
198. A rank below Mukhtiyar (Prime Minister). This rank was the prerogative of the royalty. But Bhimsen Thapa was favoured by Rana Bahadur Shah.
199. Acharya, *General Bhimsen Thapa ...*, n. 116, p. 28.
200. Whelpton, *A History of Nepal*, n. 3, p. 42.
201. Acharya, *General Bhimsen Thapa ...*, n. 116, p. 30.
202. Acharya, pp. 288-289.
203. Bhattarai, Umesh K., *Conflict to Peace: Transition in Nepal*, New Delhi: _______, 2014, p. 82.
204. Acharya, *General Bhimsen Thapa ...*, n. 116, p. 63.
205. Bhattarai, *Conflict to Peace: Transition in Nepal*, n. 130, p. 82.

Bhimsen Thapa's atrocities stand out like a sore thumb in Nepali history. He terrorised the whole nation with the help of 6000 core military under his direct command. He not only massacred his opponents but captured the entire bureaucracy under his control.[206] He lost the war with the British in 1814 and was later blamed for political naïveté.[207] Historians are still disagreed on whether he was a genuine patriot or a traitor.[208]

Nevertheless, Bhimsen Thapa succeeded in strengthening the army to be able to continue the westward expansion. The British overreach had been evident for some time after Rana Bahadur Shah was forced to conclude a treaty in 1802 and accept the resident in Kathmandu. From then onwards, the former king and his regime, largely under a team including Bhimsen Thapa, concentrated on strengthening the army, which was going through a financial crisis due to the continuing war with Tibet and China from 1788 to 1792. He modified the policy of rent-free land grants (*kusa-birta*) and gave Tarai land contracts for five years to army officers. With this policy, new army units were formed.[209]

In terms of military ventures, the British were invading from south-east towards west. Nepal was also expanding in the same direction. A collision was inevitable as both sides were westbound in a thrust to place them squarely athwart the trade routes through the Himalayas to Tibet.[210] The Nepali Army was well-trained in mountain warfare. Meanwhile, its expansionary moves were checked by King Ranjit Singh of Punjab in the Sutlej in the west. The British stopped their expansion in south, north and east. They found it not practical because of the connection Tibet and Bhutan enjoyed with the Chinese emperor (Nepal had signed a treaty with China to this effect in 1792).[211] The army was already geared up for a campaign. Therefore, postponing an expansion campaign would be economically wasteful and also demoralise the nation. The Himalayan foothills were the Nepalis' strongest line of defence.[212] Prithvi Narayan Shah in his *Dibya Upadesh* had instructed his army to fight in the hills and avoid the plains.

---

206. Acharya, *General Bhimsen Thapa ...*, n. 116, p. 42.
207. Ibid., p. 18.
208. Bhattarai, *Conflict to Peace: Transition in Nepal,* n. 130, p. 18.
209. Rose, *Nepal: Strategy for Survival*, n. 6, p. 80.
210. Stiller, *The Rise of the House of Gorkha*, n. 32, p. 286.
211. Ibid., p. 289.
212. Ibid., p. 290.

The British knew that the Gorkhalis had built up a powerful military machine in the hills and would fight with determination. Their policy was to defend the limited trails, occupying strong positions in the dominating hills. The invading forces would be deterred from learning the secret trails and passes. Initially, after Kinloch's attempt to invade Nepal in 1767, the British were convinced not to engage in war with it.[213] But while they tried to engage Nepal through envoys and residents, they constantly kept the country under surveillance.[214] Their trade with Nepal flagged and they could not explore Tibet. Also, border disputes erupted in some districts in Tarai between the two powers and the Company government laid its claim to Sheoraj and Butwal on March 11, 1814.[215]

Captain Knox, who was the Company government's first resident Nepal, had reported in 1802 that China would not take exception to British intervention in Nepal.[216] Colonel William Kirkpatrick, the second resident, had come out with a report revealing the secrets of the hills in Nepal and descriptions of Nepal's fortifications.[217] The Committee of Cargo at Canton suggested proceeding with a campaign against Nepal to ensure the preservation of the Company's China trade.[218]

When the Napoleonic war was going on, the British were compelled to concentrate their forces at home. From 1805 to 1814, their policy remained to hold the territories in India and not to engage in new hostilities. Before 1805, they were heavily engaged in battle with the Marathas in central India and against Ranjit Singh in Punjab. But by 1814 the tide had turned in favour of the British: Napoleon had been exiled and a large well-trained British army was available for service elsewhere.[219]

Under Bhimsen Thapa's premiership the Nepali Durbar took up the challenges of war with the British for three reasons. First, the British knowledge of the secrets of the hills, second, the state of army's preparedness and third, there was the possibility of powerful Indian princes siding with Nepal to defeat the British and perhaps even to drive them out of India.[220] But Bhimsen

213. Ibid., p. 283.
214. Ibid.
215. Rose, *Nepal: Strategy for Survival*, n. 6, p. 84.
216. Ibid., p. 83.
217. Stiller, *The Rise of the House of Gorkha*, n. 32, p. 288.
218. Rose, *Nepal: Strategy for Survival*, n. 6, p. 84.
219. Ibid., p. 82.
220. Stiller, *The Rise of the House of Gorkha*, n. 32, p. 288.

Thapa misread his own weakness in firepower. The Nepali Army was short in artillery. The Company was not only well-equipped but also had an excellent communication network. The Nepali line of communication was on the other hand stretched over 700 miles of mountain terrain.[221]

Nepal had either conquered or brought into an alliance the hill territory up to the Sutlej River except Kangra, which was under King Sansar Chand.[222] By 1809, all of Sansar Chand's kingdom was conquered except his capital Kangra. This was the major obstacle left for Gorkhalis to reach the valley of Kashmir, which at that time was independent, faction-ridden and ripe for the plucking by any determined aggressor.[223]

Sansar Chand had asked Ranjit Singh to safeguard his territory from falling into the hands of Gorkhalis. But Ranjit Singh had concluded a treaty with the Company government in 1809 not to claim the hill sectors in the Himalayas and even east of Sutlej. The British were also convinced that without Ranjit Singh's support, there would be no alliance with the Gorkhalis.[224] But Ranjit Singh did not wish to alienate the Gorkhalis, considering the British threat to his domain and suggested an alliance with the Gorkha, under which the Sutlej would become their boundary in the hill area. Amar Singh Thapa, the Nepali commander, recommended Ranjit Singh's proposal, but the Nepali Durbar rejected it.[225]

It then became clear that Ranjit Singh would not allow the Gorkhali to cross the Sutlej and the British would launch an offensive to confine them to the Himalayas east of the river. The Nepali Durbar had meanwhile neglected strengthening the administrative mechanism to support the war in the west.[226] The endeavour should have been to administer best practices that were set by King Prithvi Narayan Shah. Bhimsen Thapa requested the Chinese for support through the Amban, but the Chinese did not have the tradition of sending their forces to fight outside their territory. The request to King Daulat Rao Shindhe of Gwalier also did not fructify.[227] In such a milieu, war with the British devastated Nepal. The reasons for the defeat were: (i) the rampant state bureaucracy and

221. Ibid., p. 290.
222. Rose, *Nepal: Strategy for Survival*, n. 6, p. 80.
223. Ibid.
224. Ibid., p. 83.
225. Ibid., p. 81.
226. Acharya, *General Bhimsen Thapa ...*, n. 116, p. 32.
227. Ibid., p. 33.

corruption; (ii) slackness in military preparedness; and (iii) failure in getting outside support.

The defeated Nepal signed a treaty with the British in 1816 but the Nepali court refused to ratify it. The British then launched an offensive under Ochterlony in February 1816.[228] Following its divide-and-rule policy, the Company offered lucrative jobs to the youths of Kumaun, Garhwal and adjoining hills and formed a separate regiment,[229] Before the end of the war, the British enrolled 4650 deserters of Nepal Army and formed First, Second, Nasiri and Sirmour battalions in addition to Kumau Battalion.[230]

Rise of Rana Autocracy

Jang Bahadur Rana gradually appeared on Nepal's political scene after the assassination of his maternal uncle, Prime Minister Mathbar Singh Thapa, in 1845. King Rajendra Bikram was weak in decision-making and the queens were divided over who should be the next king. Jung Bahadur was a close military aide to Crown Prince Surendra Bikram Shah. King Rajendra made the younger Queen Rajya Laxmi his attorney after the death of the elder Queen Samrajya Laxmi, the mother of Crown Prince Surendra Shah.[231]

Box 2.6: The powers of attorney transferred in 1842

1. Right to imprison, expel, and death penalty to all excluding the royalty.
2. Right to recruit, post, promote and demote all state service holders.
3. Plenipotentiary right to decide Nepal's relations with China, the British and Tibet.
4. Right to declare war and emergency.

Source: Buddhi Lal Bhandari, Jung Bahadur Kunwar: Jiban Britant, p. 51.

Queen Rajya Laxmi wanted to make her son Ranendra the next king, which was against the tradition of the Nepali court.[232] She tried to get Mathbar Singh Thapa, Mukhtiyar and Prime Minister, to assent to her proposal, but failed. This led to his assassination. The queen used Jung Bahadur and Gagan Singh

228. Stiller, *The Rise of the House of Gorkha*, n. 32, p. 314.
229. Acharya. *General Bhimsen Thapa ...*, n. 116, p. 35.
230. Banskota, Purusottam, *Bidesi Sena ma Nepali Jawan Haru* (ed.), in *Military History of Nepal (Part I)*, Royal Nepal Army Headquarters, 1992, pp. 228-229.
231. Bhandari, Buddhi Lal, *Junga Bahadur Kunwar: Jiwan Britanta,* _____: Oriental Publications, 2014, p. 51.
232. Ibid., p. 61.

Bhandari to carry out her plot. The king also approved of the plot.[233] As a reward for carrying out the plot, both were promoted to the post of general in the army. Gagan Singh Bhandari was given command of seven regiments and Jung Bahadur of three regiments.[234] Later, Jung Bahadur suspected designing a plot for Gagan Singh Bhandari's murder in 1846.

At that time, the East India Company was fighting against Ranjit Singh for its survival in India. Ranjit Singh requested for military support from Nepal. Gagan Singh Bhandari and Jung Bahadur opposed the proposal whereas the rest of the court was in favour.[235] Finally, the two generals' opinion prevailed.

Jung Bahadur emerged to power after eliminating Gagan Singh Bhandari and Prime Minister Fateh Jung Shah and 30 other courtiers in the Kot massacre on the night of 14 September 1846.[236] Jung Bahadur was then crowned as Shree 3 Maharaj.[237] King Surendra Bikram merely became a pawn of the newly crowned minister.[238]

Jung Bahadur was aware of the Chinese decline of power and knew that Peking was neither willing nor able to challenge the British in the Himalayan area. He therefore inclined Nepal's foreign policy to please British India. Immediately after assuming premiership, he visited the British envoy in Kathmandu and assured him that his regime would be friendly with the British.[239] His family's autocratic rule established a new feudal model and culture in Nepal's political system.[240] He promulgated the first law called General Code on 6 January 1854, which is considered to have been the first official document of its kind.

Jung Bahadur visited England and France in 1850 for almost a year and returned with a fresh appreciation of the British might.[241] Nepal's relations with China in his tenure were strained to the extent that the customary five-year mission to that country was cancelled. China's power had been weakened after

233. Ibid., p. 69.
234. Ibid., pp. 78-79.
235. Ibid.
236. Raj, Prakash A., *Jung Bahadur Kunwar Rana ko Jiwani,* ______: Makalu Prakasan Griha, 2014, p. 14.
237. Ibid., p. 40.
238. Rose, *Nepal: Strategy for Survival,* n. 6, p. 106.
239. Bhandari, *Junga Bahadur Kunwar ...,* n. 158, p. 90.
240. Ibid., p. 92.
241. Rose, *Nepal: Strategy for Survival,* n. 6, p. 107.

the Taiping rebellion. China was also suspicious about his visit to Europe.[242] But he was shrewd enough to realise that keeping good relations with Peking would help in keeping the British at arm's length. However, in 1854, the Nepali joint mission composed of political and commercial delegates to China was mistreated in Tibet. Leo E. Rose wrote that the mission had carried opium worth nearly Rs. 300,000 to sell in China despite the ban on the entry of opium there.[243] The death of the head of the delegates also created suspicion on both sides. Nepal then decided to launch an offensive on China for three avowed reasons: (i) Tibet was having a border dispute with Nepal in the Kodari region; (ii) the grazing area south of Himalaya sold by Tibet to Nepal was resettled by Tibetans; and (iii) the mistreatment of the Nepali delegates.[244]

Since 1792, when the China-Nepal agreement was signed, Nepal had followed a non-interventionist position vis-à-vis Tibet. With Jung Bahadur's emergence, Nepal was somewhat stable. China's Qing dynasty was heavily engaged with the Taiping rebels. The British concentrated on the war with Russia on the Crimean front and Tibet had internal disturbances with the death of the sixth Panchen Lama.[245]

The Nepal-Tibet War of 1856 was not a full-blown war, as some historians like Dilli Raman Regmi do not consider it to have been one, because Kuti and Kerong were already Nepal's territory.[246] The war concluded with an agreement in Thapathali of Kathmandu with some financial benefits to Nepal through customs concessional entry to Nepali products in Tibet. But more of it was advantageous to the British.[247] Leo E. Rose agreed that Clause 4 was included at the request of the British, acting on behalf of Maharaja Gulab Singh of Kashmir to rescue Sikhs, presumably Dogras, who had been made prisoner in 1841.

242. Ibid.
243. Ibid., p. 108.
244. Raj, *Jung Bahadur Kunwar Rana ko Jiwani,* n. 163, p. 44.
245. Ibid., p. 109.
246. Raj, *Jung Bahadur Kunwar Rana ko Jiwani,* n. 163, p. 45.
247. Ibid.

Box 2.7: Summary of the Draft Agreement after the Nepal-Tibet War, 1856

1. The Tibetan government agreed to make an annual payment of Rs. 10,000 to Nepal.
2. Nepal promised to come to the aid of Tibet if it was attacked.
3. Lhasa agreed not to levy duties on commodities brought into Tibet by Nepali subjects.
4. Tibet consented to return the Sikh prisoners who had been captured in the 1841 war between Tibet and the Dogra ruler of Kashmir, and Nepal agreed to return all Tibetan prisoners. Nepal also was to withdraw from the Tibetan territory it had occupied.
5. Nepal would be permitted to install a "Bharadar" (envoy) in Lhasa.
6. Nepal was granted the right to establish a trading establishment at Lhasa for sale of all kinds of merchandise.
7. The Nepal representative at Lhasa was granted the right to adjudicate disputes between Nepalis, Kashmiris and other non-Tibetans in Lhasa. When the subjects of Nepal and Tibet were involved in a dispute, the two authorities would jointly settle the case.
8. The two governments agreed to the mutual surrender of murderers.
9. Tibet was made responsible for the life and property of Nepali subjects in Lhasa. Nepal was made responsible for the protection of Tibetans in Nepal.
10. The persons and property of subjects of Nepal or Tibet who had collaborated with the enemy during the war were to be respected by both governments.

Source: Leo E. Rose, pp. 114-115.

Jang Bahadur himself led the force against the first independence war waged against the British colonisers in North India in 1857.[248] It took three months to suppress the rebellion. Jang Bahadur met Governor General Lord Canning in Allahabad on March 23, 1858, who agreed to return four districts of western Tarai, which are the lifeline of the western hills of Nepal.[249] Jung also accepted honours and medals from the British, which no prime minister had done before.[250]

Gorkha Recuitment and Jung Bahadur

The recruitment of Nepalis into the British Indian Army had started in 1815 when a large proportion of the Nepali force surrendered after the battle of Malaun. Mostly Garhwalis and Kumaunis were recruited in the British service.[251] During

248. Ibid. pp. 46-47.
249. Ibid.
250. Ibid., p. 49.
251. Rose, *Nepal: Strategy for Survival*, n. 6, p. 132.

the war, the British were keen to use defectors and employ them as irregular forces. David Ochterlony, then commander of the British forces and Political Agent William Fraser, quickly recognised the potential of the Nepali soldiers and in April 1815, they proposed forming a battalion under Lieutenant Rose. It was first called Nasiri Regiment and was later renamed as first King George's Own Gurkha Rifles. About 5000 men entered British service in 1815, from which three battalions were formed. Initially, the recruits were from outside of Nepal proper but later Khas, Magar and Gurung communities of western Nepal enrolled into it. The magnificent fighting qualities of these battalions were quickly recognised by the British after their successful employment in the siege of Bharatpur in 1826.[252]

The British Resident in Kathmandu, Brian Hodgson, tried hard to persuade the Nepali durbar to allow full recruitment of Gorkhas in the British Army but the durbar had a standing prohibition against Nepalis serving in the British Indian Army. The durbar could not fully control the recruitment, but applied harassing techniques against British agents. Jang Bahadur also imposed stricter regulations regarding the recruitment of Nepalis into the British Indian Army.

Gorkhas from Nepal served under the British at first in the armies of the East India Company and then the British Indian Army. Their terms and conditions of service were laid down by the British Indian authorities without reference to the British government.[253] In 1947, when India became independent from the British, it was decided between the two governments to split the Gorkha regiments between the British and Indian armies. Six Gorkha units became part of the new Indian Army and four were transferred to the British Army.[254] There was to be a ceiling of 3,500 Gorkhas serving with the British Army and 40,000 in the Indian Army.

Upon Nepal's defeat in the war with the British in 1816, the Peace Treaty of Sughauli permitted Nepalis to volunteer for service in the East India Company's army.[255] But recruitment had already been in process in the middle of the war. Although Nepal had to compromise its national interest because of its lengthy

252. Ibid.
253. Britain-India-Nepal Tripartite Agreement, https://www.revolvy.com/main/index.php?s=Britain%E2%80%93India%E2%80%93Nepal%20Tripartite%20Agreement&item_type=topic
254. Ibid.
255. The British Army Website. http://www.army.mod.uk/gurkhas/27856.aspx-

lines of communication and weakness in administering the conquered areas, the British attracted fifth columnists to join their army, encouraging them to betray Nepal's nationhood at large.

Jung Bahadur resisted the recruitment process in 1858, ordering that "no subject of the four classes and thirty-six castes of our country shall go to India for recruitment without any prior approval." Punishment for disobedience was confiscation of property.[256] The British were outraged with him and suspended direct recruitment for some time but continued later.

Nepal's image of bravery and loyalty in the international arena has been mixed. During the Falkland War with Argentina, the British portrayed the Gorkha troops as "man-eaters". The terms and conditions of the Gorkhas' employment allow the British to deploy them anywhere in the world in favour of British interest, but the way the Gorkhas are re-employed in service to guard the royalty of Brunei Darussalam under the British establishment is not acceptable. Nepal has a tripartite treaty with the UK and India, and Brunei Darussalam is not a party to the treaty. Even the Indian Vice President Mohammad Hamid Ansari proposed, during his visit in February 2015, security of service of Gorkha troops serving in the Indian Army can be deputed to Brunei.[257] In the present world order, nothing can be kept secret. Secret deals are a matter of outdated history.

In the wake of the voice of ex- British-Gorka troops against the discrimination on pay and other facilities by the British establishment, PM K. P. Oli Sharma raised the concern with outgoing British PM Teresa May on June 12, 2019 while he was visiting Europe to attend the general meeting of the International Labour Organization in Geneva. He categorically proposed his counterpart to review the 1947 Tripartite Gorkha Recuitment Treaty that has the base of 202-years-old Nepal-Britain relations. This is the first time that a Nepali prime-minister as executive government head has proposed for review.[258] But the "Joint Communiqué" on behalf of the Britain failed to mention their response on Nepali prime-minster's review request. As this is a sensitive issue, it will definitely raise a debate among the intellectuals concerned.

256. Rose, *Nepal: Strategy for Survival*, n. 6, p. 133.
257. Poudel, Purusottam, Khumchido Antar-rastriya Sakh. http://www.annapurnapost.com/news/61574-
258. https://www.onlinekhabar.com/2019/06/773005#.XQDtBxmvTrI.facebook

As PM Oli had officially proposed for review of the 1950 Indo-Nepal Friendship Treaty forming the eminent persons group has not yielded any result due to Indian reluctances, this case may also be ended accordingly. But in reality, the discrimination to the British-Gorkha troops is comparatively higher than the Indian-Gorkhas in pay and pension who served prior to 1997 at the par with native British troops. In either way, the proposal will exert a pressure to both the British and Indian establishments to review after 72 years of tripartite treaty in place.

Nepal-Britain-India's Tripartite Gorkha Recruitment Treaty(1947) was concluded at the eve of Indian independence. As per Gorkha Military historian Rajesh Rai reveals that Nepal was compelled to sign this treaty under pressure.[259] Gurkha Army Ex-Servicemen's Organization (GAESO) had submitted a copy of this treaty to the Supreme Court of Britain that accepted as treaty was unequal, insulting and illegal, hence ordered the concern to make pay and pension equal as per the British troops. But still the discrimination prevails in other forms and manifestations. Let us see what will be the result of the Nepali prime-minister's review proposal in the days to come.

At the home front, other than the remittance received—there is no information of extra ransom amount that Government of Nepal has received from the British and the Indian establishments in lieu of allowing Gorkha recruitments to them. There is no substantive advantage to the national economy other than direct foreign employment that has indirectly eroded Nepali nationhood in particular. Nepal's autocratic rulers had never revealed the internal dealings that they could have made for support to them. In the lack of sufficient transparency, there is suspicion over the loyalty of such leaders in the society.

259. Ibid.

Chapter Six

Struggle for Democracy

First Popular Revolution 1950

The end of World War II and the emerging wave of democracy all over the world against imperialist power encouraged the Nepalis to speak for their rights. In the next-door, India's independence from the British in 1947 and the creation of Pakistan on religious grounds further encouraged them to abolish the Rana autocracy. The monarchy put up with the democratic forces as it had no executive power at all. The Indian establishment also supported the democratic forces. The First Revolution took place in Nepal in 1950.

Later on, however, Nepali society was embroiled in power-sharing politics; the wish of democracy was hard nut to crack. In fact, democracy is costly for a society which is closed and traditional. The Nepali society is not only underdeveloped but is multi-ethnic in character. Ideological differences have ruined the fabric of democracy. Most intelligentsia believe that King Prithvi Narayan Shah could integrate Nepal geographically, but he failed to unite the country in terms of overcoming the divisions based on ethnicity, religion, language, class and culture.

King Prithvi Narayan Shah did have a vision for Nepal, as exemplified in his *Divya Upadesh*, but his untimely death at the age of 51 was a setback in uniting Nepal culturally. His successors, excluding Bahadur Shah, did not follow in his footsteps that time. Bahadur Shah devoted his life to expanding Nepal geographically but did not pay attention to strengthening it internally. Almost all of Nepal's rulers were focused on strengthening the country's military capacity rather than enhancing administration and management to develop infrastructure and education, which are the backbone of a nation.

Bhimsen Thapa, Jung Bahadur and Chandra Shumser, though they cannot be compared with King Prithvi Narayan Shah in terms of his contribution to Nepal's development, were successful in stabilising the nation through significant reforms in their time.[260] Bhimsen Thapa modernised the military. Jung Bahadur

260. Raj, Prakash A., *Jung Bahadur Kunwar Rana ko Jiwani*: Makalu Prakasan Griha, 2014, p. 67.

promulgated the first civil code, "*Mulki Ain*" in 1854,[261] which was inspired by his exposure to the British Empire's use of codification. Chandra Shumser abolished the *Sati pratha* (burning of widow on her husband's funeral pyre) and slavery.[262] The three legends ruled Nepal for almost 30 years each, but their reign was mired in controversy.

The autocratic Ranas captured power because of the Shah kings' indulgence in luxury, reluctance to educate the citizens and empower them with their rights. It was the changing democratic wave in India that induced King Tribhuvan, who was virtually imprisoned by the Rana Prime Minister, to remove his blinkers. His anti-Rana activities in the 1930s and 40s led to their downfall in 1950. In November 1950, the king and his family sought asylum at the Indian Embassy in Kathmandu, and were later flown to India.[263]

Until their ouster, the Ranas entirely controlled the military and there was no question of the military uprising in favour of the Shah kings. It was King Tribhuvan's seeking asylum in India that divided the public opinion against the Ranas. The Nepali Congress was offering armed resistance to the Ranas with its *Mukti Sena,* but it received only limited support from India, which was apprehensive of an unstable northern frontier.[264]

To undermine King Tribhuvan's political status, the Rana Prime Minister Mohan Shumser declared the infant Prince Gyanendra, King Tribhuvan's middle grandson, as the new king of Nepal. But the Indian government was fully confident of undermining the Ranas' political standing.[265] The British envoy in Kathmandu accepted Prince Gyanendra as king, because the British were riled with the stand of Matrika Prasad Koirala, then president of the Nepali Congress, against Gorkha recruitment by the British.[266]

In the Delhi Settlement of 1951, the Nepali Congress party was mostly excluded from the preceding negotiations.[267] Delhi was not sure of the party's

---

261. Bleie, Tone, *The Decade of Violent Destabilization in Nepal,* p. 53.
262. Raj, *Jung Bahadur Kunwar Rana ko Jiwani*, p. 67.
263. Bleie, *The Decade of Violent Destabilization in Nepal,* n. 2, p. 56.
264. Tone Bleie quotes Leo E. Rose (*Nepal: Strategy for Survival,* London: University of California Press, 1971, pp. 191-192) to the effect that the refugee King Tribhuvan, under guidance from the Indian authorities, did not come out with a public statement in favour of the Nepali Congress and its Mukti Sena. The Indian authorities also placed restrictions on Mukti Sena's movement in Indian territory.
265. Gautam, Rajesh, *Nepal ko Prajatantrik Andolan Ra Nepali Congress,* 1998, p. 405.
266. Ibid.
267. Bleie, *The Decade of Violent Destabilization in Nepal,* n. 2, p. 56.

capability to be a ruling party and also feared its possible collaboration with the Nepali Communist Party at the time of the communist takeover in China.[268] Delhi therefore went for a carefully guided transition based on power-sharing arrangements through a coalition government of the Ranas, the king and the Nepali Congress.[269]

The Delhi Settlement asserted the king to be the source of power, Rana as nominal head and the Nepali Congress as coalition partner with other parties. The Army was restructured in 1952 and the *Mukti Sena* was absorbed in 1961 into it. The reverberations of this settlement are still being felt in Nepal's political development, including the present wrangling in the country.

What governing factors obstructed Nepal's stability? Was it the military? Was it the political breakthrough still deficient in democratic values? After the Delhi Settlement, the Nepali Congress's elbowroom to bargain for real democratisation was severely limited. The settlement was largely made by Indian actors in New Delhi, some of whom had multiple economic, kinship-based and ideological links with the Shah and the Ranas.[270] The two Koirala brothers, Matrika Prasad and Bisheswar Prasad, were at the top to decide the country's fate on behalf of the Nepali Congress party. Despite B. P. Koirala's repeated request to meet Bijaya Shumser, who was representing the Ranas in the Delhi Settlement, M. P. Koirala, who was party president, was reluctant to meet Shumser. B. P. Koirala wanted to clarify from Shumser why the Ranas chose Delhi for negotiation and why not Kathmandu itself.[271]

M. P. Koirala, who had strong royalist leanings – many considered him to be a stooge of the monarchy – had close ties with the 1950s generation of leadership, who were culturally acclimatised in India.[272] The Delhi Settlement empowered the king rather than the people. M. P. Koirala was appointed Prime Minister by the king in 1952. The Delhi Settlement was flatly rejected by Kuwar Indrajit Singh and his followers in the mid-western region of Nepal.

In Nepal's transitional history of democracy, K. I. Singh played a yeoman role. Born in an elite family of the Doti in Western Nepal, he completed Senior

268. Rose, Leo E., *Nepal: Strategy for Survival*, London: University of California Press, 1971, p. 194.
269. Ibid.
270. Bleie, *The Decade of Violent Destabilization in Nepal*, n. 2, p. 57.
271. Gautam, *Nepal ko Prajatantrik Andolan Ra Nepali Congress*, n. 6, pp. 454-455.
272. Bleie, *The Decade of Violent Destabilization in Nepal*, n. 2, p. 58.

Cambridge education in British India, joined the British Army and later qualified in MBBS from Calcutta.[273] He was deployed on the Burma front to render medical service to the war-wounded in World War II. Inspired by Subhash Chandra Bose, he joined the Azad Hind Force and fought for independence in India.[274]

During the first popular uprising of 1950 against the Rana autocracy, K. I. Singh was with the Nepali Congress and led the front in near-Western Nepal of Bhairahawa and Butwal region. He was critical of the Nehru-led Indian government's mediation in Nepal's democratic transition and declined to recognise the Delhi Settlement. He refused to lay down weapons[275] and moved north towards China. King Tribhuvan, apprehending further deterioration of the situation, sent General Nara Shumser with a letter, asking him to surrender and join the mainstream politics, with an assurance that his viewpoint would be listened to. Shumser met him in Dhorpatan, northwest of Pokhara, along with more than a thousand militias. K. I. Singh agreed to return to Kathmandu, but was imprisoned at Singha Durbar, which is now the state secretariat of the Government of Nepal. K. I. Singh then motivated the entire *Raksha Dal* guards responsible for defending Singha Durbar to rebel against the government forces loyal to M. P. Koirala.[276] He then left Kathmandu for Beijing and remained in exile as a guest of Mao Zedong until he was called by King Mahendra in 1957 to assume the post of Prime Minister. From this episode, Nepal should have learnt the lesson that negotiations on internal issues must be settled by internal forces inside their own territory and not subject to the dictates of another country.

Integration of Mukti Sena into the Nepal Army

In spite of agreeing to the Delhi Settlement of 1951, the Ranas obstructed its implementation, seeking to strengthen their networks in the state apparatus and obstructing the integration of the *Mukti Sena* in the Army as well as its reintegration into society. Army factions loyal to the Ranas formed a group, calling themselves as *Gorkha Dal*. Its secretary-general Bharat Shumser Rana was later arrested on a charge of planning a coup against the new government.[277] The

273. Based on an interview with Gagan Raj Bhatta, a close ally and Congress co-partner of Dr. K. I. Singh on 29 December 2016.
274. Ibid.
275. Ibid.
276. Ibid.
277. Whelpton, John, *A History of Nepal*, Cambridge University Press, 2015, p. 87.

Mukti Sena's integration was further delayed because of the trust deficit between King Tribhuvan and the democratic alliance.

King Tribhuvan then invited the Nepali Congress to form a single-party government, but he would not accept B. P. Koirala, who was the most popular leader among the party workers, as Prime Minister.[278] Much turmoil followed thereafter.[279]

In any case, after almost 11 years of wrangling, the Government of Nepal decided to address the *Mukti Sena*'s concerns in 1961.[280] The *Mukti Sena* numbered 8000 at the time. Possibly, many *Mukti Sena* members would have reintegrated themselves into Nepali society in the interim, after futilely waiting for stabilised political conditions and for the formation of stable governments that could address their concerns. Out of the total *Mukti Sena* members at the time, 3000 were integrated into the *Raksha Dal* and 5000 were enrolled into the Police. Many would have preferred to join the Army, but did not meet the requirements for recruitment. Freedom fighters who did not wish to join in the integration process – numbering 300 – were provided (Nepali) Rupees 2000 per person as compensation for their service. After 15 years of the first revolutionary uprising, the *Raksha Dal* was merged into the Army in three battalions, namely Pasupati Prasad, Singhanath and Barda Bahadur Battalion.[281]

The *Mukti Sena* was first converted into *Raksha Dal,* a para-militia structure. This group revolted in favour of K. I. Singh and two other leaders of the Kirati secessionist organisation, releasing them from prison. These three leaders then fled to Tibet.[282] There was a similar revolt in February 1951, when K. I. Singh refused to lay down arms in protest against the Delhi Settlement. The government then invited the Indian Army in the mid-Western region of Nepal, called *Bhairahawa.* The Rana hardliners had formed the *Gorkha Dal,* which was creating havoc against the newly formed government.[283] Due to poor communication facilities and non-availability of road connections to the rest of the country from Kathmandu, the Army was partly dysfunctional. Part of the reason for its poor professional performance was the feudal orientation of the

278. Ibid., p. 89.
279. Bleie, Tone, "A forgotten history, Part I and II", *The Kathmandu Post,* __________.
280. Ibid.
281. Ibid.
282. Whelpton, *A History of Nepal,* n. 18, p. 89.
283. Ibid., p. 87.

Rana officer corps, which compelled the government to invite the Indian Army to intervene in the country's military affairs. It is possible that this compulsion delayed the integration of the *Mukti Sena* (alias *Raksha Dal*) into the Nepal Army.

Compared to integrating the *Mukti Sena,* the Maoist ex-combatants' integration into the Nepal Army was much smoother, apparently. In the latter case, the international practice of disarmament, demobilisation and reintegration (DDR) was applied. Under-qualified ex-combatants and child soldiers were reintegrated into society with compensation, which several of the beneficiaries regard as having been fair. Qualified ex-combatants (whose professional competencies were highly regarded) who joined the Army totalled 1395. It may be noted that a few of them have even served with the UN peacekeeping missions abroad.[284]

Use of Military to Quell Democracy Movement 1960

King Tribhuvan leaned on India for its interventionist role. King Mahendra on the other hand pursued geopolitics to manage both of Nepal's neighbours for Nepal's own benefit. He had closely observed the entire transition of the Rana autocracy to a multi-party democracy and the wrangling of party leaders to come to power. He had witnessed the Delhi Settlement and the activities of Rana's *Gorkha Dal* and K. I. Singh's United Democratic Party. John Whelpton writes that he funded the United Democratic Party because K. I. Singh was a radical with a Robin Hood image for his anti-India and pro-Chinese leanings.

King Tribhuvan had earlier consistently ignored the Communist Party's demand to draft a new constitution by a constituent assembly. Mahendra followed in his footsteps. Instead of constituent assembly elections, he conducted parliamentary elections in 1958. The Nepali Congress won the election and formed the government under B. P. Koirala. Although the Congress had relatively closer ties with India, B. P. desired to avoid entanglement in the growing tension between India and China after the revolt in Tibet and the Dalai Lama's flight to India in March 1959.[285]

Nevertheless, the government decided to double the defence budget in order to secure the northern border and also agreed to the continuous presence of the

284. Based on an interview with Nepal Army Spokesperson Brig. Gen. Tara Bahadur Karki on 26 December 2016.

285. Whelpton, *A History of Nepal*, n. 18, p. 96.

Indian Army that monitors there. China made conciliatory moves, and Nepal abstained in the UN resolution of 1959 censuring China's conduct.[286] And B. P. subsequently rejected the idea of a defence pact between India and Nepal. But later a new dispute arose with China laying claim to Mt. Everest. Perhaps, it could be a deliberate move to counter the public preoccupation with an alleged threat from India.

Amidst the prevailing confusion, King Mahendra, using his emergency powers and control of the army, detained the Prime Minister and his colleagues at a public meeting in December 1960, citing the government's failure to maintain law and order, increasing corruption and for encouraging anti-national elements. The leaders who escaped then started a serious military campaign under Subarna Shumser. A guerrilla force, around 3000 strong, which was formed with the help of activists who fled to India, launched raids across the border.[287] The campaign further escalated when Mahendra signed an agreement with China for the construction of the Araniko Highway connecting Kathmandu with the Tibetan border town of Tatopani. The Congress activists were tagged as "anti-national" and the military was massively mobilised to crush their movement.[288] A total of 77 insurgents, 31 security forces and 22 civilians were killed in one year in the ensuing skirmishes.[289]

King Mahendra then banned all political parties and imposed a so-called Party-less Panchayat system. The system followed the "guided" democracy then existing in Pakistan, Egypt, Indonesia and Yugoslavia. Control of the military and power to impose emergency remained with the monarchy. With some modification in the constitution, King Birendra continued his father's model of political system.

Deployment of the Nepal Army against the Khampa Insurgents

After the Dalai Lama's exile to India in 1959, more than 100,000 Tibetans followed him. Despite some differences with India, Nepal's foreign policy was mainly consistent. The Tibet issue became a sensitive part of the Nepal-China relations. Dalai Lama, on exile also formed an army called "Four River and Six Mountain Range Religion Protection Army," which operated on Nepal's

286. Ibid.
287. Ibid., p. 99.
288. Bleie, *The Decade of Violent Destabilization in Nepal,* n. 2, p. 60.
289. Ibid.

northern border in the Tibetan territory against the Chinese authority.[290] The CIA supported them, initially via Gilgit in Pakistan-occupied Kashmir and later, through East Pakistan. Bruce Riedel in his book *JFK's Forgotten Crisis* reveals that CIA used Mustang of Nepal as a base to support the Tibetan Khampa insurgents to operate against the Chinese authority in Tibet. The CIA used to train them in Colorado, the state's terrain being similar to that of Tibet. To quell the Khampa rebellion, China requested Nepal's support, for which the Nepal Army was deployed for three months in Western Nepal.[291]

The case is still critical due to the US and Indian meddling to weaken China. Nepal has principally followed "One-China Policy" that does not allow it to play against Chinese policy over Tibet. The free exit of Tibetans to Dharamashala (where Dalai Lama presently resides in India) via Nepal's territory without official permit is restricted as per bilateral agreements. US, India and the Westerns advocate to allow Tibetans to enter Nepal and be freely flown to anywhere they like on humanitarian grounds. This makes Nepal on an awkward position in front of China. To overcome out from such a position, Nepal needs to follow a vibrant neutral foreign policy and firm to implement it.

---

290. *Military History of Nepal, Part II*, p. 646.
291. Whelpton, *A History of Nepal*, n. 18, p. 103.

Chapter Seven

End of Cold War

End of Cold War and Nepal's Stability

After Mikhail Gorbachev propounded his doctrines of "perestroika" and "glasnost" to bring about changes in the legacy of the Soviet Union, the new wave not only demolished the Berlin Wall and unified the two Germanys, but the Soviet Union itself disintegrated. In China, after Mao's death, his legacy of communism gave way to Deng's policy of entering the market system. India's foreign policy too changed from non-alignment to globalisation. Nepal was also swept into these tides of change.

Until then, Nepal's Party-less Panchayat system – in which mainstream political parties were banned – was controlled by the monarchy with a strong military back-up. In tandem with the world trends, popular unrest geared up in the country gradually. In 1991, there was a Second Revolution in Nepal, which was led by the Nepali Congress with the support of the left forces to sweep the Party-less Panchayat system, diminishing the monarchy to constitutional head. It took 30 years to restore popular rights in this manner in terms of restoring the multi-party system. To enable Nepal to enter the free market economy, the country entered the World Trade Organisation in 2004. Nepal's economy was looking up, but the political environment remained sullied. To clear the environment, the Prime Minster dissolved Parliament which had absolute majority of its own in the house, and called a mid-term poll.

The flavour of democracy shines with effective service of its public institutions. Public institutions must be responsible and accountable to deliver public goods and services. The people pay tax to the government in the hope that it will look after their security and maintain essential services. The Nepali Congress party was given the mandate to form the government many times after 1990, but could not meet popular aspirations.

There could be several reasons why the Maoists raised weapons against the government, but the question is why the government could not work to empower the people and strengthen public institutions. The Nepali Congress party claims to have a pluralist approach and socialist thinking, but its leadership was neither visionary nor had the political will to implement public policy.

Wrangling to Manage the Nepal Army in a Democratic Setup

In such a milieu, the Nepal Army was also not properly guided by the leadership to keep pace with its civilian counterparts for national development. The National Security Council (NSC) was envisaged by the Constitution of 1991 but its role was limited to army mobilisation. The governments were reluctant to activate the NSC effectively until 1996, when the Maoists threatened their legitimacy. In between, then Prime Minister Girija Prasad Koirala, also holding the portfolio of defence minister, tried to mobilise the army against the Maoists.[292] But he failed due to palace wrangling into it. The people's elected body was neglected many times in the history of Nepal.

In the Interim Constitution of 2006, the NSC's composition was enlarged, with the Home Minister and three other ministers to be nominated by the Prime Minister, but the army chief was not included. The constitution of 2015 also fails to recognise the NSC as an autonomous body responsible for the security of the nation. National security must ensure the development of the nation, and confirm to its values. It must also guarantee human security and the nation's territorial integrity, sovereignty, independence and freedom of action. To ensure this role, the NSC must be structured accordingly. To support it, there must be effective defence institutions at both governmental and non-governmental levels.[293]

The Constitution of 2015 has added a few more members to the NSC but does not include the opposition leader as a member. There is also no National Security Adviser. Rather, the Defence Secretary, who is not a security expert, has been made coordinator of the council. With its structure dominated by the Defence Ministry, the NSC thus looks like a defence council rather than a security council. Unless the feudal mindset is changed in the defence bureaucracy and the entire system becomes inclusive, the military alone cannot ensure national security.

---

292. The Constitution of Nepal, 1990, provided for a National Security Council, composed of the Prime Minister as chairman and the Defence Minister and the Chief of the Army Staff as members.

293. Bhattarai, Umesh K., "Suraksha Anusandhan Ka Chunauti", Annapurna Post Daily, http://www.annapurnapost.com/news/56216

PM K. P. Sharma Oli's recent decision to suspend the constitutional provision of NSC to mobilize the Nepal Army has drawn flakes on political consensus. His wish to mobilize the Nepal Army on his sole proposal to the president who presently belongs to his own party has divided the lawmakers in two distinct groups. Failure to garner a full support in the matters of national security will definitely draw a clear-cut line that may create confusion and mistrust in national unity which will be grave loss to nation building at large.

Role of UN Peacekeeping in Enhance Nepal's Image

The Nepal Army commenced United Nations peacekeeping operations through an Observer Mission in Lebanon in 1958. The history of contingent support to the United Nations started with the UN Emergency Force-II (UNEF-II) in the Sinai desert to monitor the Israel-Egypt cease-fire in 1974. Nepal continued its contribution to the UN Interim Force in Lebanon (UNIFIL) from 1978 up to the end of 2000, with some break in between due to the referendum and other domestic affairs in 1980.[294]

Nepal resumed its troop contribution to UNIFIL from 2003 and remained in the list of top five contributors most of the time. It is also recognised as the best troop provider in terms of neutrality and discipline. The Nepali soldiers have proved to be most loyal, professional and dedicated in this cause of maintaining international peace. The opening of the Birendra Peace Operations Training Centre in 2001 at Panchkhal in Kavre District has paid significant dividends in this field.[295]

Nevertheless, there were some unsavoury incidents, when a few senior officers failed in their command duties, as for example, in the UN Protection Force (UNPROFOR) mission in the erstwhile Yugoslavia and in UNIFIL Lebanon. The commanding officers in these cases failed to clear in time the troops' expectations on reward and salary, damaging the image of the institution and of the country. Similarly, for supplying ammunition to Hizbulla, an armed outfit, the battalion commander of the Nepali contingent in UNIFIL faced trial at home and was sacked from office in 2000.[296]

---

294. Bhattarai, Umesh K., *Conflict to Peace: Transition in Nepal*, 2014, ________: ___________, p. 21.
295. Ibid.
296. Ibid.

Contribution to Nature Conservation and Wildlife Protection

Nepal's geography is vivid in terms of topography and blessed with varied flora and fauna. Its virgin land after 1960 witnessed mass scale deforestation. At present, forest occupies only 25.4 percent of total land and deforestation is rampant.[297] In the period between 2000 and 2005, Nepal lost 2640 square kilometre of forest alone. This was the period when the Maoist insurgency was in the height and popular revolt against the monarchy took shape.

To control deforestation and protect wildlife, the Nepal Army was tasked in 1975 with specified mission to safeguard endangered species, plants and the natural heritage. Presently, 12 out of 22 protected forests are guarded by Nepal Army's 12 battalions and independent companies with 6778 troops covering total area around 9767 square kilometres.

In addition to all endangered species, protection of rhinos is the significant achievement the Nepal Army has so far garnered in this field. In the late 1960s, the total count of rhinos was limited to hundreds and by 2000—it reached to more than 500. Although the anti-poaching operations were going on, the demand of internal security duties constrained conservation efforts of the army during the Maoist rebellion which resulted to the decline of the number of rhinos in 2005. But in the year 2011, 2013 and 2015; Nepal could celebrate "zero poaching year" as well.

Infrastructure Development

Although the Nepal Army was involved for the purpose of nation-building from the day of its inception, it was tasked to construct a road "Kanti-Raj Path" after Nepal entered into the democratic process after the Rana autocracy in 1959. "Tribhuvan Raj Path" connecting the Kathmandu valley to Southern Tarai was built with Indian support and was first of its kind where the the Nepal Army and Indian Army worked together. With much generosity, the Nepal Army is continuously supporting mainly to open the pilot tracks in the remote hilly regions where the civilian contractors are not willing to work. It is not only the most cost-effective and dedicated bodies but also has trained its manpower and resources in support of the national progress for many decades.

As it has been instrumental in opening up remote areas through rugged mountainous terrain with a large number of roads and bridging projects, the

297. Nepal Army website: http://www.nepalarmy.mil.np/bpd.php?pg=envcon

national planners are comfortable to work with. The selfless sacrifices of army personnel and its institutional drive and integrity have made it possible for them to maximize the benefits from limited resources. As per Nepal Army's website,[298] the major infrastructure developments carried out are listed in Annex "A" attached.

Disaster Management

Nepal Army is a competent national force prepared to meet the full spectrum of challenges to security and defense. Besides conventional duties that are assigned, it is well-prepared and fully competent in carrying out rescue and reconstruction of natural disaster and calamities. In the past, it had effectively contributed to support civilian authority to disaster management. Its geography as well as being in high seismic zone, has high risk from natural calamities. On several occasions, in response to both natural and man-made disasters, the Nepal Army has mobilized its well-trained and highly skilled manpower in rescue missions and has succeeded in saving lives and property of the population under risk.

The mega earthquake of 1934, the earthquake of 1988 with its epicentre in Udayapur, the massive floods of 1993 in the central region of Nepal, the flooding in the Koshi Barrage area in 2008, the epidemic in Jajarkot in 2009, the massive landslide in Jure of Sindhupalchowk and the avalanche and blizzards in the western mountainous region in 2014 are some of the major disasters where the Nepal Army was mobilized in rescue and relief operations.[299]

The Nepal Army has also been involved in international rescue and relief operations. It was mobilized in rescue and relief operations after the devastating earthquake in Haiti in 2010 and has had to take on such responsibilities in other United Nations mission areas also. Similarly, air assets from the Nepal Army's Aviation Wing were sent to supply relief materials when a devastating earthquake hit Pakistan in 2005. Likewise, in 2011, after a devastating earthquake struck Japan, a 12-member search and rescue team from the Nepal Army was put on standby.[300]

The mega earthquake of April 2015 was a most devastating and government was confused about how to manage rescue. Initially, the Disaster management Committee under Home Ministry could not take lead as confusion persisted in

298. http://www.nepalarmy.mil.np/bpd.php?page=one
299. http://www.nepalarmy.mil.np/opssankatmochan/english_part1.pdf
300. Ibid.

the civilian bureaucracy. The Interim Constitution of Nepal 2006 was in force that time. Although it provisioned to mobilize the army for disaster management without prior authorization of the parliament, the government was confused by misinterpreting existing law. The current Constitution of Nepal also follows the same line. The lesson learnt of last rescue and reconstruction could be a best example to simplify our system and not to let political meddling into disaster management at all.

Autocratic Legacy in the Military

The Nepal Army was formed, groomed and cared for by the Shah rulers and was seldom misused. But later on, Bhimsen Thapa used his 6000-strong core military group to terrorise his opponents.[301] Similarly, Jung Bahadur Rana deployed his core group of *Bijuli Garat* to massacre his opponents at Kot Parba.

The military has an important role in ensuring the democratic process. Hence, it should be given a concrete role and responsibility. The civilian control should decide on the matter, but the modality to implement security plans should be given to the security bodies. But in Nepal, the monarch being the patron and supreme commander of the armed forces, has failed to adhere to the principle of civilian supremacy. King Mahendra, for example, though he is considered to have been the most patriotic, nationalist and visionary, failed to run the state as per the democratic process.

He was conservative to restore democracy and liberalisation. His foreign policy was biased towards India and he played the China card at times. His conservative image was diluted due to his success in enabling Nepal to gain UN membership in 1955 despite the reservation of the Soviet Union. The military was under his direct control and the Army Act of 1961 granted him absolute power over the military. His son Birendra followed in his father's footsteps but was compelled to become constitutional head after the Second Popular Revolt in 1989-90. After the massacre of his family, King Gyanendra's ambition of becoming an absolute power paved the way to oust the monarchy from Nepal through the Third Popular Revolt in 2005.

During the period of total war, the military remained the only mechanism for the rulers to exercise power. The main source of state revenue was land and was limited to military expenditure. The warlords used to be the virtual

301. Dhungel, Ramesh, *Swadhinta Ra Desh Bhakti Ko Apabakhya, Kantipur Daily*, 2010, p. 6.

rulers, unaccountable to the people. The military's loyalty was confined to pleasing the rulers rather than ensuring human security. It is generally agreed that as an institution, the Nepal Army has always remained loyal to the ruling dispensation.[302] General Rookmangad Katwal also notes that the Nepal Army is continuously performing the duties assigned by the legitimate regime and as per the law of the land.[303] It is nevertheless a fact that autocratic rulers have misused the army for their vested interests. This is a reminder that unless the public institutions are strengthened, the rules are vulnerable to being trampled down.

302. Nayak, Nihar, "The Nepal Army at the Crossroads" in Vishal Chandra (ed.), *India's Neighbourhood: The Armies of South Asia,* New Delhi: IDSA, 2013, p. 97.
303. *Military History of Nepal* (*Vol. 2*), 2008, Foreword.

Chapter Eight

Post Maoists War

Solidarity between the Maoists and the Democratic Parties

The Maoists waged war commencing in 1996, with 40 demands. The Nepal Army was dragged into the conflict when the Maoists attacked the Dang barrack and captured a large cache of arms, ammunition and explosives. The government declared the Maoists, a terrorist outfit and announced bounties for decimating them and red corner notices in 2001. The Terrorist and Disruptive Act 2001 came into existence as a sunset and sunrise type of law to deploy the army against them. In the Army's counter-insurgency war, more than 17,000 people died, three times that number was wounded and more than 50,000 disappeared. The child soldiers deployed by the Maoists, who were left unattended, are contributing heavily to the crime graph in the urban areas of Nepal.

In the initial phase of the insurgency, the Army was slow in delivering results. It was committed in the battle almost after 40 years (fought insurgency battle against the *Mukti Sena,* an armed faction of the Nepali Congress, in 1960). The government, led by then Prime Minister Sher Bahadur Deuba, had international support to fight against the Maoists, but King Gyanendra fired him on the grounds of incompetence. As a consequence, the international support to the royal regime declined.

King Gyanendra had a two-front war to tackle the hostilities in the country. One was the ongoing armed conflict. The other was the democratic alliance of the seven mainstream political parties. The international community did not support the second battlefront. In solidarity with the popular concern, the democratic alliance collaborated with the insurgents. The Maoists thrived on this support at a time when they were losing the battle against the army.

The 12-Point Agreement between the Maoists and the Seven Party Alliance paved the ground for a republican state although it was not the Maoist agenda and creation of a Constituent Assembly to promulgate the new constitution by the people themselves. Ceasefire was immediately imposed and the Maoists were confined to designated camps set up by the government. The army remained in the barracks till the election was over and the registration and verification of Maoist combatants and their arms were completed.

Reasons for Prolonging the Democratic Transition

Political violence is endemic around the world. Political violence has been a common phenomenon to suppress the people's aspirations for democracy and for a say in how they want to be governed. David Rapoport's four-waves theory of modern international terrorism has been further elaborated by Jeffrey Kaplan as the fifth wave, which he says a party like Khmer Rouge in Cambodia converted into a full-fledged practitioner of regime terror.[304] It is said that the diaspora jolt the nation to drive the main political course in the right direction. The Nepali Maoists were also moving in the same direction as the Khmer Rouge initially, but gave up violence gradually, except the Netra Bikram Chand faction. The present Nepal Communist Government with an ex-Maoist in it is behaving similarly like the Khmer Rouge of Cambodia in Nepal.

In fact, Nepal's second constituent assembly could only deliver the new constitution in 2015, but stability was prolonged due to the political parties' failure in garnering consensus to the three-tier elections envisaged by the constitution. Also, the constitution had not been owned by the Madhesis and some factions of *Janajati* initially. They want the constitution to be amended before conducting elections, but the second-largest party, then United Marxist Leninist was in opposition, had declined that demand.

Prof. S. D. Muni, a Nepal expert of India has revealed that immediately after the second constituent assembly elections, the party leaders had a tendency, after fighting other factions, used to go to the palace and seek the king's advice when there was monarchy in Nepal. This betrayed their lack of self-confidence. And now, when there is no monarchy, they are seeking third-party intervention to solve their problems and that is India now.[305] Due to the cultural affiliation, they were more comfortable consulting the Indian establishment and other close allies rather than opting for Chinese suggestions. But now, this tendency is gradually changing.

Although the Nepal Army had fewer intakes in the prevailing political setup, stability was a major concern for it as tasked by the constitution. Country

304. Kaplan, Jeffrey, *Terrorism's Fifth Wave: A Theory, a Conundrum and a Dilemma*,2008.
305. Bhattarai, Umesh K., *Conflict to Peace: Transition in Nepal,* New Delhi: Adarsh Books, 2014, pp. 270-271.

was prevalent with violent political upheavals by Maoist uprising followed by Madhesi agitation in 2007. The agitation sparked off with demand of regional autonomy, right of self-determination and single Madhes province.[306]

The uprising can be graded separately from Madhesi point of view, but it did not only take lives and property but also divided social cohesion and disturbed the entire fabrics of social harmony. It was against the government and the mainstream political parties, who hastily ousted monarchy and declared a republic in Nepal. The pictures projected were like it was the demand of the people, but in reality - the leaders of the mainstream political parties were influenced by the international power centres to compromise its religion, culture in the social front and federal states against the geopolitics of this nation.

The Madhesi people are aware of their political rights, hence united as well as allied to many other Madhesi parties into one to form strong representation in the house. In first Constituent Assembly Election, their united front could become fourth largest party but in second election they slipped down. As it was needs of the time to reconcile from prolong conflict, the High-Level Political Committee (HLPC) was formed to guide the non-elected government by the political appointees. It was in place when Chief Justice Khil Raj Regmi was the head of the Council of Ministers to conduct second election of constituent assembly (CA). The debate sparked off to continue even after the elected government and equation of power changed in the house.

The Nepal Army remained in the barracks during the first CA election. But in second election later, it was tasked to confirm security as well. In some of the places like Nuwakot, Nepal Army was blamed to be part of rigging and supporting government to manipulate election results. Prakash Chandra Lohani, RPP leader was in the lead to protest the army's role as biased.

After along debate, the HLPC was decided to continue as an oversight to an elected government. The Maoist party was dominant in the HLPC, who blocked the Rastriya Prajatantra Party (RPP) though it could garner the fourth position in the second CA election. The Madhesi front, although it was slipped down was included in the HLPC. This remained the matter of contention in the house which led to mistrust in the implementation of the Constitution in Nepal.

Federalism has remained a hard nut to crack. As we all know, it is a system of the government whose sovereignty is divided between a central governing

306. Social Science Baha. http://soscbaha.org/kumar-khadka/

authorities and constituent political units like state and provinces. But the NCP Government has not still accepted federal norms practically. In fact, it matters not only on geographical demarcations but also on the distribution of resources. The present tussle is embroiled mainly between the NCP and the Madhesi front on the amendment bill pending at the house.

The Tikapur incident where seven police officers were killed ignited federal issue to different elevation. The popular uprising in Butwal and Nawalparasi sector was another example on which the Puspa Kamal Dahal's government wanted some portion to be adjusted between No. 4 and No. 5 Pradesh, respectively. The contention still prevails politically in that sector.

As a consequence, the implementation of entire constitution is wrangled on how the provincial states and their local governments could be functional; the demand of - *ek Madhes ek Pradesh* - is adjusted. The bickering activities of the political parties had raised suspicion on their success to stability. In the wake of such frustration, the popular aspiration had turned to other power centres which they hope could stabilize the nation. Out of some, could be the ousted monarchy, the army or any other power that is trying to establish like Biplav under cover. People suspect that if the Maoist can come to power then why would Biplav not come if its agenda is approved by the people.

To analyze credible power centres, we must understand the geopolitics of the region. The way - *Madhesh* - was highlighted at some point was perhaps due to its character to become a 'buffer inside the buffer' in the manner in which Nepal is a buffer to India and China, it can be between "Hill Nepal to North India". This is a very sensitive issue from the Nepali integration perspective.

Power-Sharing Alignments

People's power is the ultimate criterion in governance and comes through the ballot. A constituency's demarcation must be scientific, based on population density and area covered. In Nepal's topography, population density is higher in the plains than in the hills. Hence, this factor needs to be balanced. The present contention on implementation of the new constitution lies in the lack of this balance.

In transitional settings, all the powers within a society try to garner advantage on their side. Emotional inclinations on some specific issues do come into play, which may lead to results in the elections that may not be in the best interests of the country. In the initial stage of the peace process, the Maoists were accusing India for being responsible for the deadlock in their progress. Prof. S. D. Muni accepts India's responsibility partially as it had strayed away from consensus, but in his view, the main fault lay with the Maoists, the Nepali Congress, the Madhesi alliance and the international community.[307] Later, then Indian Ambassador Jayant Prasad in the South Asian Forum for Policy Studies on February 15, 2012 pointed out that there was the monarchical power too, which Muni missed out.[308]

The monarchical power is trying to get into the politics gradually. The failure of political parties to transform Nepal into the democratic set-up through a manipulated two-third majority, the present Government of NCP under PM Oli is becoming a simple majority (after withdrawal of the Sanghiya Forum and the RJP party that supported NCP) is a symbol to the eroding ethics of transparency as well as the rampant corruption insisting neutral people incline towards old system. The Nepal Army as had been supportive long to the royalty is seldom dragged into controversy although it is cautious to present political culture. The disintegration movement started by personalities likes C. K. Raut in Tarai had challenged openly the territorial integrity of this country has been brought into the mainstream politics under the grand design of the NCP Government of PM K. P. Sharma Oli.

It was really a surprise of the Oli Government that concluded 11-Point Agreement with C. K. Raut, Coordinator of Alliance for Independent Madhes to withdraw its demand for separate state. C. K. Raut renounced party's demand by entering 11-Points Agreements that Oli Government readily agreed upon. What miracle had happened with C. K. Raut that he easily gave up year's long demand without substantive gain? It has been suspected that PM Oli and his team could reach a fresh agreement with the European Union and the West since the time his government agreed to sponsor the Asia Pacific Summit of the Universal Peace Federation from November 30 to December 3, 2018 in Nepal.

Most Nepali media had blamed this summit as a grand design to spread Christianity in Nepal. C. K. Raut had been alleged with the European Union and the West from the very beginning of his campaign for separate state. This agreement has surprised many as why he surrendered all of sudden or it was a

307. Ibid. Bhattarai, p. 208.
308. Ibid.

charismatic approach of PM Oli that he could establish an effective nexus with the Europeans through the Universal Peace Federation. After coming to the mainstream, C. K. Raut's Janamat Party contested by-election in December 2019 where party's turnout was horrible. This shows how popular he is in Nepal and especially in Madhesh.

A recently published online report reveals that the one-time Maoist child soldier Lenin Bista has petitioned a file against the Nepali establishment at the United Nations Council for Human Rights just at the eve of PM K. P. Sharma Oli's visit to attend the International Labor Organization general meeting on June 9, 2019.[309] As per the report, the file petitioned against the Government of Nepal failure to guarantee the human rights and justice of the victims. It has been complained that the government is mute to activate Truth and Reconciliation Commission effectively as the leadership of the Maoist party are ruling the nation including Puspa Kamal Dahal as one of the NCP party chairmen now.

It has already been proved that the Maoist party had extensively employed child soldiers in its people's war against the Nepali establishment. A victim of Maoist forceful entry in its military cadre named Sita Tamang (by the changed name Manju Gurung), who was just 13-years-old that time criticized the party and the leaders at the United Nations Security Council. As per the report published in the *Himal Patrika* (*Kantipur Daily*, July 5, 2010), she was not only a single child soldier who was forcefully recruited by the Maoist.[310]

Despite of ILO Convention 182 prohibiting to employ child soldiers including Security Council Resolutions 1261 (1999), 1314 (2000), 1379 (2001) and 1460 (2003), the Maoist party had extensively employed more than 3000 child soldiers aging less than 18 years when peace deal was signed in 2006. The child soldiers were released into the society with just NRs 10,000/- equivalent to USD 140/- that time instead of the state providing formal schooling and vocational training. This was the compensation to these children who spent their formative years inside the rebel structure, losing out the critical skills which could have been vital for their adulthood.[311]

With such mindset of the Nepali leaders—its politics is mired up with selfish interest as how they can influence the power centres and remain in the regime. It

309. http://pahilopustak.com/news/view?id=19571
310. Bhattarai, Umesh K., *Conflict to Peace: Transition in Nepal,* New Delhi: Adarsh Books, 2014, p-67.
311. Ibid. pp 231-32.

is not only with the child soldiers—there are many other issues where leaders are playing with the people's sentiment. Presently, a fresh development is ongoing in the NCP leadership to leg pulling between two chairmen PM Oli and Puspa Kamal Dahal for next premiership. PM Oli is trying to please European Union against Nepal's national interest. Side by side, he is trying to deal other power centres like USA as well as neighbouring powers India and China, respectively. As the Nepali media has already smelt the conspiracy, both are trying to grab regime as per their hidden agreement concluded when their parties the UML and the Maoist decided to unify into one as the NCP.

PM Oli is said to be discrediting his counterpart Prachand to the extent to be trailed at the International Criminal Court on the charges of genocide that he committed during a decade long Maoist insurgency in Nepal. This blame at the Nepali media has not been verified independently from other sources yet so far. Besides of such meddling, the present constitution is itself vague enough to allow the ruling government to play with its provisions. Depending upon the structure of the proportionate and FPTP members of the house, there is almost no possibility of a majority government formed by a single party unless manipulation takes place just as what the present NCP Government has done to forge alliance with other parties.

Military Dogma in the Nepali Politics

The political will-power and decision-making is influenced by the socio-economic condition of the country. As the Nepal Army being is apolitical institution in nature, it cannot be inclined to any of it, but leaning of its leadership cannot be ruled out. In any event of such leaning is open, the stability has been jeopardized. Such events had been seen and felt when rulers like Bhimsen Thapa and Jung Bahadur used the army to fulfill their vested interest. But, at present—check and balance is adhered and no military leadership can openly show their leanings in the political affairs of the country. So, the military is gravely united into one and no political parties can claim loyalty of military leadership leaning to them at large.

In the political arena, the parties are severely divided to each other. Unless the electoral system is revised and threshold imposed to fringe parties at one side and ratio of the proportionate candidates are decreased considerably at the other—no majority government can be formed. The coalition culture demands proper power sharing arrangements to stable the entire system as politics is overriding to all. Military at times guards and suggest the political bodies when and where the stability is threatened. The present situation in Nepal is passing through those circumstances as province and local governments are fragile, opinions severely divided on secularism forcing disintegrating forces to unite against the cohesiveness of the country.

Inclusiveness, Professionalism and Democracy in the Nepal Army

Every army has its own strength and weakness. Depending upon the threat and capacity; state decides its size, composition, and mandate. State also needs to manage resources and budget to maintain it. Nepal Army is not exception to this. It had largely a closed structure in the Panchayat regime. Even after the political change in 1990, the Nepali politicians and the government failed to regulate, monitor and oversight the army. They perceived army was formed and groomed to fulfill the interest of the palace only.[312]

The governments formed under the multi-party system after 1990 did not pay enough attention to improve governance, empower people through ideal decentralized local bodies and strengthen public institutions at one side, they failed to own army as credible national institution and restructure it as per national character at other side. The situation has not yet been improved when the new constitution is in place and provinces and local governments are formed after the three-tiers of elections concluded almost two years ago. In fact, the Nepal Army gravely remained under the palace and its Principal Military Secretary in the Panchayat era. Now the civilian supremacy over the military has been endured but an effective control is still on limbo. There was confusion as well as lack of confidence in the political leadership on how to govern the military in a democratic setup. Basically, the schooling of the military in the autocratic setup was also different compared to an open democratic environment.

The family centric military leadership was reluctant to follow democratic norms and values. It was enjoying in the gross structure of army formed by King Prithvi Narayan Shah who composed it on existing tribes, class, gender under service categorized as who should be the officers, soldiers and also like cobbler, washer man, tailor, and blacksmith. The Nepal Army was later patterned to the British model but the working ethics and the mindset remained primitive.

312. Uprety, Bishnu Raj. *Restructuring Nepal Army: A Conflict Transformation Perspective.*

Instead to modernize the army, leadership after 1990 found it a hard nut to crack as it being directly under the palace in a constitutional monarchy.

In the mean time, the Nepal Army was tasked to quell insurgency waged by the Maoist in 2001. The insurgency ended after 12-Point Agreement in 2005 with fresh debate geared up to restructuring, inclusiveness, professionalism and democracy in the army. The question in its national character and civil supremacy were much hiked. As a consequence, the Interim Constitution-2007 envisaged reservation for under representation of various ethnic tribes and caste and marginalized groups in the public service which enabled Nepal Army to follow 45 percent of all vacant positions to be reserved for them in which 20 percent are for women, 32 percent are for Janajati, 28 percent are for Madheshi, 15 percent are for Dalit and 5 percent are for remote regions. The comparative details about the state of caste and ethnic inclusiveness in the Nepal Army based on the population and the total representation in this institution are shown in Appendix "B" attached.

Notwithstanding the fact that the army is merely a tool of national security among variety of other tools in addressing complex threat—the political leaders were against it as it was wrongly used to suppress democratic political process by the palace. Without visualizing the context, they were demanding to restore civil supremacy in mobilizing and controlling the Nepal Army. As "little knowledge" is dangerous, they were unanimously demanding to democratize it. In their understanding, democracy in the army also meant to opening of "trade unions" as in the corporate houses as they did with the civil bureaucracy who is almost defunct to its working ethics now.

The deserters in the Nepal Army are another complex case to be solved. They are high in number who left the army when it was fighting intense insurgency battle with the Maoist. This number counts as high as 12,310 including 54 officers, 27 Junior Commissioned Officers and rest other ranks and followers. They are demanding to be reinstated in the army. At times, they had organized themselves and showed their solidarity as they were not allowed to return to duties because of the Maoist pressure to their families and the environment was as such that they were compelled to be deserters. But law cannot be challenged. The Nepal Army is insisting to take actions who failed to discharge duty as per the existing Military Act - 2006 as well.

Democratizing the military means making it functional through rule of law. Professionalizing is a process of training to make it accountable and responsible towards the popular regime. If the regime is not popular itself, it cannot insist military alone to function as per the rule of law.[313] There is one school of thought that believes that the meaning of democracy does not entirely apply in the military. The mission-oriented training and professionalization of the army meet the requirement of the democratic norms and values if it is well-structured and guided properly. Army is such an organization which sets it standard in terms of professional efficiency depending upon the mission it has to implement.[314] But lack of will-power to reform the military in top political leadership as well as the army itself has prolong the popular wish to restructure this institution to become more inclusive, people-oriented and dependable organization.

Political Wrangling in Military Leadership

There has been a long debate for and against civil supremacy over the military in Nepal. After the country's entry to republic, the political leaders had no knowledge to manage military in democratic setup. And they were also not ready to listen to military leadership due to long antipathy against each other. Basically, the political leaders had trust deficit towards the military as it had long association with the monarchy. The advocates of civilian oversight were also unclear about how to establish a link between the military and the civilian counter parts. In fact, the National Security Council composed of ministers who are political representatives of the parties had no technical knowledge to manage the military.

The dismissal case of General Rookmangad Katwal by the first Maoist-led government is most controversial in Nepal's history. The tumbling of government is a matter of research for many social scientists in a country which is not only geographically sensitive but also a victim of divergent ideology that cripple the entire fabrics of national integration into peril.[315] The case can be interpreted from different angle but the country's transition has been prolonged due to trust deficit at both ends.

313. Bhattarai, Umesh Kumar. *Conflict to Peace: Transition in Nepal*. P.126.
314. Thapa, Rajendra. *Sena Bisayak Swet-Patra, Tasbir ko Bagh*. Annapurna Post.
315. Bhattarai, Umesh K (Brig Gen). *Politics and Military Leadership: A case in republican Nepal.* http://lokaantar.com/en/articles/politics-and-military-leadership-a-case-in-republican-nepal/

The brouhaha had started with the date of birth case of General Katwal with Second-in-Command Lieutenant General Kul Bahadur Khadka. As being next in the hierarchy, his desire to replace him cannot be taken as an "unnatural" step. The date of birth case was filed in the Supreme Court (SC) which took almost three years to get the final verdict and even months were taken to get the "sheet-roll" from the Army Headquarters to the SC which is not even at one-mile distance to each other.[316] Senior Advocate Biswa Kanta Mainali accepted this as the SC was quite liberal on the cases of politically motivated corruption compared to others. Designed by military leadership, the SC dismissed the case later when Katwal retired as the Chief of Army Staff.[317]

The dismissal case of Katwal from the Chief of Army Staff by the then Maoist-led government was stopped by the prerogative order of the President Ram Baran Yadav. It was later accepted by the SC as president's order did not fall within the framework of its jurisdiction and right to dismiss him remained with the government. In this connection, Advocate Khim Lal Devkota viewed as the politics in Nepal would have gone differently if the court had not denied justice in the case of Katwal's date of birth and defined the president's move was wrong that time.[318]

The case was quite embroiled and indicating towards India's micro-management in Nepal's domestic affairs. As per Katwal's "Autobiography" he mentioned that after the dismissal, he contacted few important personalities over the phone while he was returning from the prime minister's residence. But he declined to reveal who those personalities were. He cited it as "state secret". Grapevine had it that he was talking to his counterpart in India and pleading to do something as the Maoist Government had dismissed him to topple the entire regime and the army as well.[319]

If such rumours are true then the question arises, is it fair to invite foreign intervention in internal matters? Being first man of the army, he was responsible to set an example in the organization but he failed to do so. As evidence, it was later accepted by India's Ex-Foreign Secretary and Ambassador to Nepal Shyam Sharan through his statement that India had interfered in Nepal's internal affairs

---

316. Basnet, Madhav. (2011). Nepal Magazine. P.23
317. Loc Cit. Bhattarai, Umesh K. *Conflict to Peace: Transition......* P.119.
318. Ibid.
319. Loc Cit. Bhattarai, Umesh K (Brig Gen). *Politics and Military Leadership: A case in republican Nepal.*

in General Katwal's dismissal case by the then government in 2009 (*Kantipur Daily*, July 28, 2012). He further revealed that it was India's wish not to let the Maoist erode the professional image of the Nepal Army at any cost.

As a consequence, the Army's image was saved but Nepal's political transition was dragged to another vicious circle of conflict. General Katwal used the SC and its machinery for his advantage and also used the Indian establishment when he felt the existing law could not protect him through the SC. In this "tug of war," the ultimate victim was the infant republic in Nepal whose peace process was not only prolonged but the new conflict embroiled into another bout of conflict between the army and the Maoist.[320]

General Chhatraman Gurung replaced General Katwal in a very controversial manner after side-lining Lieutenant General Kul Bahadur Khadka whose image was fully tarnished as a traitor by General Katwal. He was made a "scapegoat" for his dismissal episode by the Maoist government. It was not unfair on the part of General Khadka to seek timely verdict by the SC in the date of birth case of Katwal which would have opened his way to become the next chief of Nepal Army. It was Katwal's responsibility to insist for a timely verdict by the SC and facilitate smooth transition to his successor. But he influenced his rank and file to prolong the case till the time he desired to remain in the post. General Gurung reveals some of the facts in his book *Janata ko Chhoro* (Son of a Commoner) as Katwal was trying to extend his tenure unethically but the Madhav Kumar Nepal-led government rejected his proposal.[321]

General Chhatraman Gurung commanded the Nepal Army in a very low profile in the beginning. He was introvert in nature but remained professional throughout his tenure. His communal feeling which he could control at the initial stage surfaced in the spontaneous way when his community insisted him to abuse power. In his tenure, he could integrate Maoist combatants into the army and stopped the much-hiked confrontation with the Maoist that was escalated during General Katwal's period. The role he played in the "Katwal Dismissal Episode" cannot be said to be neutral as he was against the government's decision, the legality of which could only be interpreted by the court in a democratic setup. As per his book, *Janata Ko Chhoro,* his intension has been clearly revealed that if he could not sideline General Kul Bahadur Khadka, he would not have become the next Chief of Army Staff after Katwal.

320. Ibid.
321. Ibid.

General Gaurab S. J. B. Rana was third in the line to become the Chief of Army Staff in republican Nepal. He was much expected by most Nepalis as he was trained and exposed to international arena more than his predecessors. His "Fast Track Promotion" system and bidding adieu of incompetent officers with golden handshake were controversial due to his failure to remain impartial in his decisions. Next on the line General Rajendra Chhetri had started his tenure managing the Madhesi agitation and five month long "economic embargo". When the normal diplomatic mechanism failed, he opened military diplomacy to convince Indian counterpart to lift the blockade which was successful. But, the Madhesi issue is a standstill till today, rather embroiled with C. K. Raut's arrest and release, respectively.

General Purna Chandra Thapa took over the post as the COAS after Chhetri who could not remain immune from corruption allegations. General Thapa's understanding and function in the army is praiseworthy till today, but how he would manage his colleagues to refrain from the corruption allegations—would be manifested in the days to come. The mega project like "Fast Track" and the army welfare projects are slowly becoming controversial as the senior officers are dragged into the corruption scandals. Unless they can clear their positions with sufficient logic, there is the possibility that General Thapa also can be the victim if he fails to keep his subordinates in right track.

The way General Thapa made public his property details for the first time in the Army's history which although mandatory to present to the government, his subordinates have not done so. Till date, there are three senior generals and officers who have followed his path to bring out the details in public. It is learnt that he has asked all the officers up to the rank of major generals to present their property details directly to him. It seems he is committed to his policy. It is of course, difficult to change the institutional culture, but a dedicated and determined commander can definitely change it.

Chapter Nine

Conclusion

Consequences of a State Failure

State is an authoritative body that is responsible to promote national interest which needs to be defined and developed by consensus. If it is not done accordingly, the state becomes fragile. There is the contention among the stakeholders of Nepal that its national values are not included to define national interest. Basically, the national interest must be well-defined, politically debated and approved by its citizens. In fact, there is trust deficit among the main stakeholders of the state. The leaders are gravely divided ideologically and unable to come to consensus. They are scared of general referendum as the popular verdict may challenge their wish.

The political culture in Nepal has the legacy of autocratic rule from the time of its inception as a modern state. They considered citizens as merely a tool to gather taxes for their luxury. In fact, Nepal's geopolitics also compelled the country to take care to please the regimes of its two giant neighbours in the south and in the north. The country's entire system was ruined after King Rana Bahadurs' period. He was assassinated by his step brother under a chronicling corruption charge. He was close to Bhimsen Thapa who is suspected by the historians that the major plot for this incident was hatched by him. Later, he became the de-facto ruler of the Regent Queen Lalit Tripura Sundari. He ruled this country for 31 years and later, compelled to suicide on a trumped charge of poisoning the young prince.

He was made the scapegoat of the entire failure to retain greater Nepal and was compelled to sign the 1816 Treaty with the East India Company, which confined the territory to Nepal's present boundary. But Jung Bahadur Rana managed to please the British by providing them military support, both lawful and unlawful. In return, he regained the lost territory of Banke, Bardiya, Kailali and Kanchanpur from the British in 1860.

Security is a prerequisite for a nation's sustainable development. The decade-long Maoist rebellion and the legacy of autocratic rule weakened the state's capacity to ensure human security. In fact, it was due to individual interest prevailing over national security interests. A nation cannot alone decide how the power centres play against its national interest. To counter such unwanted powers, nation has to develop strength to overcome it. The geopolitics of a nation is a major factor that dictates its challenges and the opportunities. The national capacity to use its geopolitics as strength depends on its intellectual capital.

Unless Nepal develops a culture to research and development in strategic studies, it will remain poor in balancing its activities in global vis-à-vis regional strategic stability. Strategic interaction through vibrant think tank is only the way to develop vision and garner opinion of like-minded intellectuals for consensus on contentious issues.

In fact, we must understand that stability of Nepal will not prevail unless we promote national integration directed to increase awareness on common identity amongst the citizens of Nepal. It is an emotional attachment as well as the sense of common belonging of the nationalism irrespective of caste, class, religion, ethnicity and language. Unity in diversity comes at the foremost when the nation is in a crisis like war or other calamities. It is the fusion of nationalism and patriotism synthesised through cohesiveness that is mapped in terms of unified integration. Extremism once radicalised negates social harmony either as ultra-nationalism or ultra-anti-nationalism. Both are destructive for national integration.

Ironically, the open border with India is not beneficial to both the countries. It is actually favoured by the smugglers and the criminals who carry out cross-border activities for illegal works. Some of the border dwellers advocate for it to promote their vested political interest. From the security point of view, it must be regulated as early as possible.

The way the westerners are spreading Christianity in Nepal and slowly the impact is transmitting towards North India—there is the possibility of Hindu and Buddhist gearing up against religious conversion. It is learnt that even Muslims are planning to convert other religions to Islam under the grand design of some gulf countries in Nepal. Siraha district under No. 2 Province is probable the conference site in the near future. As India is launching a champaign against the Muslims under the BJP Government, it is likely that they may use the open-border to spread their religion through Nepal.

China is also plagued of religion conversion on its majority Han community by Christianity at large. If such forceful conversion is not stopped, there is the possibility of mass resentment in the entire region. If Nepal fails to recover from the present fragility, its close neighbours will definitely experience a spillover effect. The rivals will try to use this opportunity to discredit us at the most. They are targeting to erode our cultural values, which are sensitive and easy to attack. If we fail to protect our society collectively, we will be the loser in this battle.

Geopolitical Sensitivity

Geopolitics is the study of the inter-dependency of geography with the politics and vice versa. In fact, international relations are dictated by geopolitics. Nepal's geopolitics is debatable as a challenge as well as an opportunity from the days of its inception. King Prithvi Narayan's *Dibya Upadesh* is the first of its kind that defines Nepal's strategy of national security vis-à-vis foreign policy. Later, King Mahendra adopted the non-alignment movement in the sixties which was guided by his philosophy.

In pursuit to this movement, King Birendra proposed Nepal to be declared a "zone of peace" in 1975 during his coronation ceremony which was his earnest desire to institutionalize peace and was also an act which was inspired by his ancestors' wish to make Nepal neutral and independent. Ironically, this proposal was a failure due to Indian resistant. In fact, the non-alignment movement is also dormant at this stage after the disintegration of the Soviet Union and end of the Cold War. The emergence of China as a global power has again surfaced the possibility of a bipolarity, once again. The Russian Federation and China are together in many international issues.

China is aggressively committed on its Belt and Road Initiative (BRI) to connect rest of the world with it. But there is the fresh debate as China is trying to lure up to trap the poor economies under its debt and use their facilities for its strategic gain. The negative reports of the BRI have confused even to its neighbours who have already signed the project. Nepal is one of them.

India is not convinced with the BRI and motives behind Chinese intensions. They have long-term dispute over border demarcation and have fought a major war in 1962. The recent Doklam incident is fresh. Although they have strong trade relations with each other and expect to increase more in the days to come but the strategic rivalry continues to show their influence in the sub-continent.

Despite of their trade interest, India does not want China's strategic involvement in South Asia.

Stability - A Basic Need to Development

In the ancient and medieval period when connectivity was really poor—the tiny and small principalities had no reach to rest of the world. The imperial powers like British East India Company and the former Soviet Union created fear among the sensitive leaders in this part of the Himalayas. The Chinese monarchy had poor control over Tibet. The real time strategist King King Prithvi Narayan Shah foresaw the future of divided principalities to counter the offensive, so decided to integrate them forming a modern state.

In fact, King Prithvi Narayan's vision is still valid in the present Nepali context. The gist of his *Dibya-Upadesh* reveals that Nepal could not only be united from his individual effort but was possible through a collective endeavour. So, he mentioned it as a garden with flowers of four tribes and thirty-six castes (*char barna* and *chhatish jaat*). Although he mentioned categorically four tribes and thirty-six castes, one should understand that he meant all natives who were residing that time in Nepal, are the same for the nation. But his *Dibya Upadesh* is wrongly interpreted by some of the contemporary leaders under the guidance of anti-national elements.

Bahadur Shah and Rajendra Laxmi followed largely the same path as Prithvi Narayan but Rana Bahadur Shah was notorious from various angles. In his tenure, Bhimsen Thapa remained centre of power as his core adviser till he was assassinated by his step-brother Sher Bahadur Shahi. After Ranamukteshor incident, Bhimsen Thapa emerged to power as the de-facto ruler under the regency of Queen Lalit Tripura Sundari as King Griban Yuddha was infant. Bhimsen Thapa seized all the powers and declared himself as first prime minister and Commander-in-Chief of Nepal. He exercised absolute autocratic rule for 31 years. Nepal was under war with the British and lost its confidence that Prithvi Narayan, Bahadur Shah and Rajendra Laxmi had so far garnered as a strong nation.

Jung Bahadur Rana emerged to power as similar as Bhimsen Thapa through bloodshed and durbar conspiracy. Jung Bahadur and his family rule lasted for 104 years. The Rana rulers pleased the British to prolong their regime. They knew how Bhimsen Thapa was trapped by the leading families contending the power by influencing the palace. He used the British to tame and control the contending powers against him.

Although Jung Bahadur was a close ally to the British, he was not in favour to allow Nepali youths to join the British Army. He resisted the recruitment process in 1858 imposing punishment defying the states' order. He was vigilant and informed about the plight of the youths will make the nation weak. The British could not openly offend with him and suspended the recruitment for some time but continued covertly.

It was Bir Shumser who allowed British to recruit the Nepalis openly. Chandra Shumser also followed him to please them. He supported the British to crash the Tibetan rebellion of 1905 in Yunnan province which is widely known as the Boxer Rebellion. The rebellion was guided against the Qing Dynasty by the Tibetan Lamas. The Qing Dynasty invited Christian missionaries to crash them. The Nepal Army took part in support of the British per se the Qing Dynasty under Chandra Shumser's order.

By the time India got its independence from the British in 1947, the wave of democracy had already started chasing Nepal's politics. Notwithstanding the changing wave, the Ranas were just in a lasting sleep when the Nepali Congress established the first political party in 1946. The monarchy was in virtual house arrest by the Rana rulers. The Rana intimidation and torture forced King Tribhuvan to establish a nexus with like-minded democrats including the Nepali Congress which was already in existence in India.

In most contemporary democracies where the system has plunged, the cases are similar as like-minded leaders followed the models that apparently look popular but in reality, they were different. In the recent past, we have seen some rulers who broke the existing system and imposed authoritarian rule as they like. The example could be of General Augusto Pinochet of Chile and President Recep Erdogan of Turkey.

Similarly, the Russian President Putin's atrocity to suppress opponents and its leaders as well as to suspicious poisoning of close rivals is few other examples. President Donald Trump's suspension of many democratic moves of the predecessors ignoring global concerns in the name of "America First" is ridicules. His national security advisers' contempt of International Criminal Court against its ruling of abuse of power of the US Army in Afghanistan that caused genocide has serious concern for the UN Security Council. Likewise, Nepali establishment's arrogance to establish Truth and Reconciliation Commission as per the international rule set by the UN apex bodies is also open challenge to human rights.

There is the tendency of the political leaders in the developing countries that once they are elected—they presume as lifetime boss of the citizens, and legitimacy to rule haphazardly. There are many who believe legitimacy is not a one-time event conferred through an election or the establishment of charismatic authority but a continuous process of deepening and broadening the rights and obligations of citizenship.

Malpractices in the Nepali Politics

Why is politics not pure? The answer is because it deals with the power - it does not remain at one place for ever. The tendency of power is to shift to those who can absorb it. The power neither sees who is ethical or not, nor by what means it is achieved—just shifts who can hold it. In one sense, politics is science of power, which cannot be achieved without capturing the regime. That is why the politicians make groups—sub-groups, manipulate the system bargaining for power with the powerful. Mergers, splits and conversions take place when politicians lack power in the existing circumstances.

Politics fall into the wider domain of the entire societal study, where human development carries an important role to play. Stability and development are complimentary to each other. Based on the geopolitical constraints of the specific location in the prevailing situation—its strength and weakness are accessed. Understanding it as knowledge is equally important to negotiate with other powers. Failing to do so—the weak has to face negative consequences. For example, Nepal has been punished several times in its history when its leaders failed to know geopolitical constraints of this country very well.

They also failed to follow it as a discipline to make lifestyle easy. Their grave negligence was to ignore the importance of connectivity that can only negotiate geopolitical constraints at large. Signing of 'Belt and Road Initiative' with China and the decision to open access to its ports is Nepal's first step to open connectivity towards the north. Once these avenues are open - Nepal's geopolitical dynamics will automatically change.

The leaders in the democratic set-up did not dare to challenge the hegemonic influence of the powerful nations. The British legacy in Nepal's bureaucracy and politicians' circle is so deep-rooted that has still not gone even after 70 years of democratic practice. India too is severely affected by such mindsets being directly ruled under colonial framework compared to Nepal. The way British used to impose its will - India wanted to establish a similar hegemonic influence from the very beginning of its independence. In the changed environment, Nepal does not want such imposition - so confrontations were frequent from the time of its first transition to democracy in 1950 till today.

The Nepali politics is mired up with selfish desires of the third grade leaders who have neither long-term vision nor the will-power to implement the programmes and projects of public needs. They are graded third because first grade youths very seldom join the politics – the second grade reach to the level to lead but compromise ideology in lieu of financial gains, so their image are faded in the crowds; the third grade have neither ideology nor integrity. They represent gangsters and encourage criminology in the politics. They control the entire system under their grip through wealth, woman and weapon.

Military Legacy and Political Culture

The ancient and medieval period of total war was purely dominated by the military. The civil administration was virtually under the military commander's control. In Nepal, even after its integration to modern state by King Prithvi Narayan Shah, its entire system was controlled by the royal families or the military commanders who were close to them. The king used to be the supreme commander of the army. He used to decide who should be the army chief and when to launch a war against which state, and conclude a treaty with any other state.

The council of ministers and the army chief managed the military affairs on the king's behalf. Military ranks and assignments were conferred by the court on the army chief's recommendation subject to the king's final approval. The rank and portfolio were primarily given on the basis of class and caste, rather than on qualification and competence. The army chief was responsible for administering routine affairs, inspecting the forts for war preparedness and for commanding active operations. This tradition was followed till the time monarchy was in power in Nepal.

Gravely, the political culture was based on favouritism and nepotism. Corruption was under control at the lowest level but at the top level—the entire public revenue was considered private property of the monarchy and their families. There were no formal education system and mass employment for the professionals. Whosoever could please the powerful—were given the lucrative positions at the state bureaucracy. Other than army, there was no such employment source to the state. When the British East India Company and King Ranjit Singh of Punjab decided to enroll Nepali youths in their army, the Nepali *durbar* got annoyed.

Gurkha recruitment in the British Indian Army is controversial from the time the East India Company started it solely in 1815. Nepal was defeated in the war with the British in 1816, consequently it had to sign the Peace Treaty of Sughauli that permitted the Nepalis to volunteer for service in the East India Company's army. But recruitment had already been in process in the middle of the war. Although Nepal had to compromise its national interest because of its lengthy lines of communication and weakness in administering the conquered areas, the British attracted fifth columnists to join their army, encouraging them to betray Nepal's nationhood at large.

Jung Bahadur resisted the recruitment process in 1858, with executive order as whoever defies will be liable to confiscation of property. The British were outraged with him and suspended direct recruitment for some time but continued later. The Nepali durbar had also imposed a standing prohibition against the Nepalis serving in the British Army, though it could not fully control it. It was Bir Shumser who allowed the British to recruit the Nepalis openly. Chandra Shumser also followed him to please them. He supported the British to crash the Tibetan rebellion of 1905 in the Yunnan province which is widely known as the Boxer Rebellion.

Meddling in Gorkha Recruitment

The Nepal-Britain-India Tripartite Gorkha Recruitment Treaty of 1947 was signed by Nepal under pressure. Gurkha Army Ex-Servicemen's Organization (GAESO) had submitted a copy of this treaty to the Supreme Court of Britain that accepted as treaty was unequal, insulting and illegal, hence ordered the concern to make pay and pension equal as per the British troops. But still the discrimination prevails in other forms and manifestations. Let us see what will be the result of the Nepali prime-minister's review proposal in the days to come.

At the home front, other than the remittance received—there is no information of extra ransom amount that Government of Nepal has received from the British and the Indian establishments in lieu of allowing Gorkha recruitments to them. To address ex-British-Gurkha's concern, PM K. P. Oli Sharma requested the outgoing British PM Teresa May on June 12, 2019 to review the 1947 Tripartite Gorkha Recuitment Treaty that has the base of a 202-years-old Nepal-Britain relations. aThis was the first time that a Nepali prime-minister as an executive head of the government has proposed for review. But the "Joint Communiqué" on behalf of the Britain failed to mention their response on the Nepali Prime Minster's review request.

Reactions after Xi's Visit to Nepal

President Xi Jinping was said to be curious to know how the Nepali state can be more stable. For this, he not only inquired about the political stability, but also, wanted to know how monarchy is settled. As it has been indicated by some reliable source, he pursued to know the role of monarchy in particular so that Nepal's stability is assured. As development being the core to strengthening democracy, his visit was focussed to interlink Nepal into its dream project BRI. For this, both agreed to become "strategic partner" for development. This has created some concern in Delhi as to how the Indo-Nepal relations will shape in the present context of the Nepal-China mindset. Some intellectuals have proposed for a new treaty but it will be wise to accept the Eminent Persons' Groups recommendation, which is pending at the moment. But still if both the countries want to further explore to accommodate their interest—they can always do so.

Findings

The Nepali state has lots of ups and downs in its history. The autocratic dictatorship has ruined the entire fabrics of democracy so far, which the state could garner when there was the benevolent dictatorship in place. Yet the Nepali durbar had played both roles on and off in its history. In the period after the democratic process in 1950, there was "political wrangling" among the leaders that experienced a setback to the infant democracy making it fall down in the hands of the palace.

The second revolution in 1990 forced the monarchy to become constitutional but the "political wrangling" again paved the root to Maoist insurgency in 1996. The third revolution in its history took place in 2006 by an alliance of seven parties and the Maoist converted Nepal into a republic state. But still, the resentment of the people is not over as the government is not able to deliver the public good and services effectively.

The inability of the government to garner stability had led the state to become fragile. In this fragility, the international power centres are playing dirty to make the environment polluted through like-minded leaders on its socio-cultural fabrics. As Nepal has cultural commonalities with its neighbours, it will be easier for their rivals to attack through it. So, India and China both should take care of Nepal, respectively.

With the recent visit of the Chinese President Xi Jinping in Nepal, the Oli led government has made some shift in its priorities. Some of the pacts signed by both the governments are meant to have long-term impacts. The India-centric developmental policies under the framework of the Indo-Nepal Friendship Treaty (1950) will definitely change as it has been already been indicated by some intellectuals in New Delhi. How the Indo-Nepal relations will develop in the changing scenario will be clear as days pass by in our calendars.

References

Acharya, Baburam, 1964. *Nepal ko Samchhipta Britant,* Kathmandu: Prof Krishna Prasad Acharya.

Acharya, Baburam, 2008. *General Bhimsen Thapa: Yin Lai Maile Jasto Dekhe,* Kathmandu: Sri Krishna Acharya.

Baidya, Tulasi Ram, 1992. *Ancient and Medieval Military History of Nepal (ed.)* in *Military History of Nepal (Part-I).* Royal Nepal Army Headquarters.

Bajracharya, B.R., 1992. *Bahadur Shah: The Regent of Nepal.* New Delhi: Anmol.

Banskota, Purusottam, 1992. *Bidesi Sena ma Nepali Jawan Haru (eds) in Military History of Nepal (Part-I).* Royal Nepal Army Headquarters.

Basnet, Madhav, 2011. "Nepali Sena", *Nepal Magazine.*

Basnett, Yurendra, 2009. *From Politicization of Grievances to Political Violence: An Analysis of the Maoist Movement in Nepal,* http://www.lse.ac.uk/internationalDevelopment/pdf/WP/WP78.pdf

Bhattarai, Baburam, 2010. "Nepali Rajniti Ko Bhabi Disha", *Kantipur Daily,* 24 March.

Bhattarai, Umesh K., 2014. *Conflict to Peace: Transition in Nepal,* New Delhi: Adarsh Books.

Bhattarai, Umesh K., 2015. "Madhesi Agitation: Comprehending Consequences on Indo-Nepal Relation", *The Diplomatist,* http://diplomatist.com/dipo201511/article001.html

Bhattarai, Umesh K., ____. "Suraksha Anusandhan Ka Chunauti", *Annapurna Post Daily,* http://www.annapurnapost.com/news/56216

Bhattarai, Umesh K. *Politics and Military Leadership: A case in the republican Nepal.* http://lokaantar.com/en/articles/politics-and-military-leadership-a-case-in-republican-nepal/

Bhattarai, Umesh K. (2018) *Demography Changes and Threat on National Security-* A paper presentation (eds) in Bharat-Nepal Relations: Defense and Security Issues. Neeti Anusandhan Pratisthan. Nepal (NeNAP).

Bleie, Tone, 2007. *The Decade of Violent Destabilization of Nepal.* Kathmandu: ______

Bulletin of the Central Department of Sociology and Anthropology, T____U_____, 2010. "A Forgotten History, Part I and II". *The Kathmandu Post,* 22/23 September.

Constitution of Nepal, 2015.

Dhungel, Ramesh, 2010. "*Swadhinta Ra Desh Bhakti Ko Apabakhya*", *Kantipur Daily,* ________.

Gautam, Rajesh, 1998. *Nepal Ko Prajatantrik Andolan Ra Nepali Congress,* Sri Ram Shrestha.

Gautam, Pradeep Kumar. (July 2016). *Understanding Dharma and Artha in Statecraft through Kautilya's Arthashastra.* IDSA, New Delhi, India *https://idsa.in/system/files/monograph/monograph53.pdf*

Kaplan, Jeffrey, 2008. *Terrorism's Fifth Wave: A Theory, a Conundrum and a Dilemma,* http://www.terrorismanalysts.com/pt/index.php/pot/article/view/26/html

Luitel, Tilak Prasad, 2016. *Koutiliya Arthsastra.* Bidhyarthi Pustak Bhandar. Kathmandu

Military History of Nepal, Vol.2, 2008.

Nayak, Nihar, 2013. "The Nepal Army at the Crossroads". In Vishal Chandra (ed.), *India's Neighbourhood: The Armies of South Asia.* New Delhi: IDSA.

Nepal, Gyanmani, 1993. *Nepal ko Mahabharat,* Kathmandu: Sajha Prakasan.

Pant, Mahesh Raj, 1966. "*Bir Bhakti Thapa*", *Purnima* Anka 10.

Rachman, Gideon, 2016. *Easternisation,* London: The Bodley Head.

Rawal, Ram Bahadur, 2011. "*Rastrabad Vs Rastraghat*", Kathmandu, *Nepal Weekly*, 13 November.

Riedel, Bruce, 2016. *JFK's Forgotten Crisis,* New Delhi: HarperCollins.

Rose, Leo E., 1971. *Nepal: Strategy for Survival.* London: University of California Press.

Sapkota, Rupak. (December 24, 2019). *नेपाल चीन कि अमेरिकातिर.* Kantipur Publications.

https://www.kantipurdaily.com/opinion/2019/01/24/154829542119824417.html

Sharma, Jagadish. (2006). Nepal: Struggle for Existence. ComnInc, ICT Private Ltd, Kathmandu, Nepal

Sun Tzu. *The Art of War.* Translated by Lionel Gils, http://classics.mit.edu/Tzu/artwar.html (Accessed on March 4, 2018.

Thapa, Karna Bahadur, 2002. *"National Security of Nepal 1990-2000, A Study of Concept, Vulnerabilities and Threats"*, Dissertation, Kathmandu, Tribhuvan University (unpublished).

Thapa, Rajendra. (2011, June 9). *Sena Bisayak Swet-Patra, Tasbir Ko Bagha.* Annapurna Post Daily.p-7.

Uprety, Bishnu Raj, 2007. *Restructuring Nepal Army: A Conflict Transformation Perspective.* Nepali Journal of Contemporary Studies Vol. VII No.1

Upadhya, Sanjaya. 2016. *Nepal and the Geostrategic Rivalry between China and India.* Routeledge. NewYork.

Whelpton, John, 2005. *A History of Nepal,* _______: Cambridge University Press.

Internet

Adhikari Bipin. (2015, March 6). The Divya Upadesh of Prithvi Narayan Shah. Spotlight Vol:08 No. 17. https://www.spotlightnepal.com/2015/03/06/the-divya-upadesh-of-prithvi-narayan-shah/ (Accessed on February 3, 2018)

Bhattarai, Umesh Kumar. *India-Nepal Relations*-Foreign Policy Research Centre, New Delhi India, Journal 19, 2014. http://www.fprc.in/Pragya-NEPAL-19.pdf

inextricably file:///C:/Users/ukbha/Downloads/New-Media-and-Its-Role-in-Stabilizing-Nepal_-A-Geopolitical-Context-Published%20(3).pdf (Accessed on April 22, 2018)

A Brief History of the British East India Company http://learn.culturalindia.net/brief-history-british-east-india-company-essay.html (Accessed on February 3, 2018)

Britain-India-Nepal Tripartite Agreement, https://www.revolvy.com/main/index.php?s=Britain%E2%80%93India%E2%80%93Nepal%20Tripartite%20Agreement&item_type=topic

The British Army Website- http://www.army.mod.uk/gurkhas/27856.aspx-

Chaudhury, Rahul Roy. (July 6, 2018). India's 'inclusive' Indo-Pacific policy seeks to balance relations with the US and China. International Institute for Strategic Studies

https://www.iiss.org/blogs/analysis/2018/07/india-inclusive-indo-pacific-policy-china-relations

http://carnegieendowment.org/2018/03/02/creating-unstable-asia-u.s.-free-and-open-indo-pacific-strategy-pub-75720

Delhi Policy Group's report on 'India and Connectivity Frameworks, November, 2017, p-11-- https://www.delhipolicygroup.org/uploads_dpg/publication_file/india-and-connectivity-frameworks-1074.pdf

Jackson Eric. Sun Tzu's 31 Best Pieces Of Leadership Advice. https://www.forbes.com/sites/ericjackson/2014/05/23/sun-tzus-33-best-pieces-of-leadership-advice/#108403d35e5e (Accessed on March 22, 2018)

Kemos, Alexander. The Influence of Thucydides in the Modern World http://www.hri.org/por/thucydides.html (Accessed on March 22, 2018)

Stiller, L.F, S.J, Father. (June 28, 1968). *Prithvi Narayan Shah in the Light of Dibya Upadesh*. Catholic Press, Ranchi, India. file:///C:/Users/ukbha/Downloads/1968%20Prithwinarayan%20Shah%20in%20the%20light%20of%20Dibya%20Upadesh%20by%20Stiller%20s.pdf (Accessed on February 10, 2018)

Why do Nepalese join the Indian Army? https://www.quora.com/Why-do-Nepalese-join-in-the-Indian-army

Purusottam Poudel. *Khumchido Antar-rastriya Sakh*. http://www.annapurnapost.com/news/61574-

Madhesi Agitation

Social Science Baha. http://soscbaha.org/kumar-khadka/

Interviews

Tri Ratna Manadhar, Professor and Ex- Vice Chancellor of Lumbini Buddhist University, Nepal. Interviewed on October 2, 2016.

Dinesh Raj Pant, Professor of Mahendra Sanskrit University and Academics at Nepal Academy, Kathmandu, A Renowned Historian of Nepal- interviewed on November 7, 2016.

Gagan Raj Bhatta, a close ally and Congress co-partner of Dr. K.I Singh and a historian; interviewed on December 29, 2016.

Brig. Gen Tara Bahadur Karki, Spokesperson Nepal Army; Interviewed on December 26, 2016.

Annex-A

(Refer to Page 47)

The Nepal Army's Contribution to Infrastructure Development

- The Nepal Army was the major partner in the old Kantipath project linking Kathmandu to the Indian border.
- It also constructed the Kharipati-Nagarkot road. Today, Nagarkot is one of the key tourist sites in Nepal.
- North West of Kathmandu, the Trishuli-Somdang road cuts through 105 Kms of extremely difficult terrain. This road was completed in 1990.
- By developing the 88 Km long Katari-Okhaldhunga Road, the people of the Everest region had the necessities of life delivered right at their door steps. This track was completed in 2005. Likewise, the 28 km long Hile-Leghuwaghat road was also constructed.
- The 86 Km long Salyan-Musikot road runs through some of the most remote and deprived parts of Nepal. The development of road would be an important catalyst to the social and economic development of the region. It was handed over to the local authorities on completion in 2005.
- The 232 Km long Surkhet-Jumla road, built in large parts by the Nepal Army has been heralded as one of the herculean development achievements in modern Nepal. Besides the construction of the road, this project incorporates various other side projects for the upliftment of the rural society through which this road passes. Rebuilding of irrigation channels, vocational trainings for the under privileged, micro hydroelectric projects have also been incorporated into this project.
- The Baglung-Beni-Jomsong road, which is 91 Km long, is built through some of the most picturesque terrain and can support the development of the region by providing transport to a region rich in agricultural products.
- The 45 Km long Drabya Shah Marga, was built with a view to combating insurgency by pursuing development and security, simultaneously. The 37 Km long Satdobato-Niwel-Balua road, the 39 Km long Gorkha-

Mankamana road and the 45 Km long Gorkha-Aarughat-Orkhet road were also built under this program.

- The Besi Sahar-Chaame road is a 65 Km long mountainous road. It follows the Marsyangdi river along the famous 'Annapurna Circuit'. This route provides service support to one of the most popular tourism areas in Nepal.
- The 107 km Chhinchu-Jajarkot road, the 112 km Jajarkot-Dolpa road, the 31 km Devsthal-Chourjahari road, the 145 Km Musikot-Burtibang road, the 91 km Nagma-Gamgadhi road are currently being built to provide access to some of the remote and least developed areas of Nepal.
- Likewise, the 81.8 km Nijgadh-Kathmandu fast track is currently being opened which is seen as an important catalyst in the connection of the Terai and the Capital city Kathmandu.

Annex-B

(Refer to Page 54)

Table 3.2: State of Castes/Ethnic Inclusions in Nepali Army

Caste/Ethnic Groups	Population (2001 Census)	% of Total Population	Represen-tation in NA	% of Represen-tation
Chhetri	3,593,496	15.80	39,824	43.6
Brahmin	2,896,477	12.74	7,634	8.36
Magar	1,622,421	7.14	6,444	7.06
Tamang	1,282,304	5.64	5,473	6.00
Newar	1,245,232	5.48	6,035	6.61
Tharu/Chaudhari/ Rajbansi	1,629,691	7.17	4,343	4.76
Gurung	543,571	2.39	3,145	3.45
Thakuri	334,120	1.47	2,967	3.25
Kami	895,954	3.94	2,488	2.73
Rai/Sunuwar	635,151	2.79	2,687	2.94
Sanyasi	199,127	0.88	2,058	2.25
Dhamai/Dholi/Gandharba	390,305	1.72	1,900	2.08
Sarki	318,989	1.40	1,034	1.13
Gharti/Bhujel	117,568	0.52	1,257	1.38
Kumal	99,389	0.44	763	0.84
Hajam/Thakur	98,169	0.43	707	0.77
Limbu	359,379	1.58	434	0.47
Majhi	72,614	0.31	325	0.36
Teli/yadav/Rajput	304,536	1.34	260	0.28
Darai	14,859	0.07	142	0.16
Sherpa/Thakali	1,80,558	0.74	120	0.13
Dusad/Paswan/Dom	158,525	0.70	124	0.13
Danuwar	53,229	0.23	104	0.11
Muslim	971,056	4.27	12	0.01
Mechhe/Tatma	3,763	0.02	47	0.05
Jerel	5,316	0.02	52	0.06
Thami	22,999	0.10	10	0.01
Chepang	52,237	0.23	9	0.01
Pahari	11,505	0.05	33	0.04
Raji	2399	0.01	06	0.00
Others			821	0.9
Total			91,258	100

***Source:** CBS for column (b) and (c) and AG Dept (Records office), Army HQ for (d) (As of April 1, 2009).*

State of Castes/Ethnic Inclusion in the Nepalese Army (As of August 26, 2016)			
S.No.	Caste/Ethnic Groups	Total Representation in NA	(%) of Total Representation in NA
(a)	(b)	(C)	(d)
1	KSHATRI	39721	43.176
2	BRAHMAN	8093	8.797
3	MAGAR	7253	7.884
4	NEWAR	5577	6.062
5	TAMANG	4934	5.363
6	THAKURI	3213	3.492
7	THARU	3021	3.284
8	KAMI	2891	3.142
9	GURUNG	2753	2.992
10	RAI	2278	2.476
11	CHAUDHARI	1773	1.927
12	JOGI	1718	1.867
13	PARIYAR	1074	1.167
14	SARKI	969	1.053
15	LIMBU	717	0.779
16	KUMAL	698	0.759
17	THAKUR	664	0.722
18	DAMAI	662	0.720
19	BHUJEL	494	0.537
20	GHARTI	373	0.405
21	NEPALI	340	0.370
22	MAJHI	273	0.297
23	SUNUWAR	262	0.285
24	YADAB	240	0.261
25	PODE	144	0.157
26	DURA	138	0.150
27	DANUWAR	126	0.137
28	DARAI	117	0.127
29	SHERPA	115	0.125
30	RAJBANSHI	114	0.124

31	RANA	89	0.097
32	DHIMAL	82	0.089
33	MADHESI	57	0.062
34	KHATWE	55	0.060
35	CHAMAR	50	0.054
36	JIREL	49	0.053
37	MAHATO	35	0.038
38	MANDAL	34	0.037
39	DHANUK	33	0.036
40	BOTE	33	0.036
41	TELI	33	0.036
42	DOM	32	0.035
43	PAHARI	31	0.034
44	MUSLIM	27	0.029
45	KASAI	24	0.026
46	MECHE	23	0.025
47	NAU	22	0.024
48	DUSADH	22	0.024
49	DHOBI	21	0.023
50	TATMA	21	0.023
51	MEHATA	19	0.021
52	SAH	19	0.021
53	HAYU	15	0.016
54	RAJPUT	15	0.016
55	CHEPANG	15	0.016
56	GAINE	14	0.015
57	KURMI	13	0.014
58	THAMI	13	0.014
59	GUPTA	13	0.014
60	BADI	13	0.014
61	TAMATA	12	0.013
62	SHAH	11	0.012
63	JHA	11	0.012
64	URAWA	10	0.011
65	KUBER	10	0.011
66	PASWAN	9	0.010

67	SADA	9	0.010
68	THAKALI	8	0.009
69	KUMAI	8	0.009
70	RAJI	8	0.009
71	MUSAHAR	8	0.009
72	KANU	7	0.008
73	DAS	6	0.007
74	LAWAD	6	0.007
75	KUSWAHA	6	0.007
76	TAJPURIYA	6	0.007
77	SUDI	5	0.005
78	SARDAR	5	0.005
79	SANTHAL	5	0.005
80	JHAGAD	5	0.005
81	OD	5	0.005
82	KAPAR	4	0.004
83	TIRUWA	4	0.004
84	CHUNARA	4	0.004
85	MALAHA	4	0.004
86	KALAR	3	0.003
87	RAJDHOB	3	0.003
88	SATAR	3	0.003
89	SAHANI	3	0.003
90	PHARSWAN	3	0.003
91	PASI	3	0.003
92	BARMA	3	0.003
93	SRIVASTAVA	3	0.003
94	DHAL	2	0.002
95	DHEGA	2	0.002
96	GURDHAMI	2	0.002
97	KEWAR	2	0.002
98	CHHANTYAL	2	0.002
99	JOHARI	2	0.002
100	KABIRATH	2	0.002
101	DAUDI	2	0.002
102	DEO	2	0.002

103	GAHATE	2	0.002
104	DEVJAN	2	0.002
105	KEWAT	2	0.002
106	SINHA	2	0.002
107	SAMAT	2	0.002
108	KUMHAR	2	0.002
109	PAWE	2	0.002
110	LODH	2	0.002
111	SUTIHAR	2	0.002
112	MAKRA	2	0.002
113	TABDAR	1	0.001
114	SUTPARAI	1	0.001
115	CHILAUNE	1	0.001
116	CHITAURE	1	0.001
117	CHUNDALI	1	0.001
118	CHUWAIN	1	0.001
119	DALA	1	0.001
120	SULI	1	0.001
121	TADI	1	0.001
122	SHEKH	1	0.001
123	CHAIHAN	1	0.001
124	DATTA	1	0.001
125	SHAHU	1	0.001
126	DAUT	1	0.001
127	DAYALE	1	0.001
128	SERMA	1	0.001
129	SAUKE	1	0.001
130	DHADI	1	0.001
131	SANWAT	1	0.001
132	SOB	1	0.001
133	BELAL	1	0.001
134	BACHHAR	1	0.001
135	WAYAK	1	0.001
136	BAG	1	0.001
137	BAHAKARI	1	0.001
138	BAITHA	1	0.001

139	BARAGHARE	1	0.001
140	BARAKOTI	1	0.001
141	BARGHARE	1	0.001
142	TITARA	1	0.001
143	BARWATI	1	0.001
144	CHANDRABAN	1	0.001
145	BEGNASI	1	0.001
146	SAITHBAR	1	0.001
147	BHIYAL	1	0.001
148	BHUJAWA	1	0.001
149	THYAITA	1	0.001
150	BHUMIHAR	1	0.001
151	THAMPHARA	1	0.001
152	TARIYA	1	0.001
153	CHACHHARA	1	0.001
154	CHADARO	1	0.001
155	RAUT KURMI	1	0.001
156	TAKMEL	1	0.001
157	BASHAHI	1	0.001
158	LOTHYAL	1	0.001
159	MUDIYARI	1	0.001
160	MEDANIYA	1	0.001
161	MARWODI	1	0.001
162	MARIK	1	0.001
163	KAHAR	1	0.001
164	KALAL	1	0.001
165	MARAU	1	0.001
166	KAMAT	1	0.001
167	MADARNIYA	1	0.001
168	ROSHYARA	1	0.001
170	NUNIYA	1	0.001
171	KAUSHA	1	0.001
172	LOPPA	1	0.001
173	LONIYA	1	0.001
174	KHADLUK	1	0.001
175	KHANG	1	0.001

176	KOHAR	1	0.001
177	KOLI	1	0.001
178	LEKHI	1	0.001
179	YOLA	1	0.001
180	ANSARI	1	0.001
181	MABO	1	0.001
182	GARANGA	1	0.001
183	KUPAR	1	0.001
184	DIYAL	1	0.001
185	KUMAR	1	0.001
186	DUMJAN	1	0.001
187	RAUB	1	0.001
188	DURAL	1	0.001
189	RAM	1	0.001
190	GADARIYA	1	0.001
191	GADERI	1	0.001
192	RAJWAR	1	0.001
193	MUDVARI	1	0.001
194	GAMAL	1	0.001
195	MURAU	1	0.001
196	GAREDI	1	0.001
197	GHARALA	1	0.001
198	PHULARA	1	0.001
199	GODIYA	1	0.001
200	GORATHOKI	1	0.001
201	GOTH	1	0.001
202	GUICHE	1	0.001
203	PELA	1	0.001
204	PABE	1	0.001
205	SAI	1	0.001
206	PODAR	1	0.001
TOTAL		91998	100.000
Source: AG Dept (Army Records Office), Army HQ			

Annex-C

(Refer to Page 10)

Bingfa (Art of War-Holding the Enemy without Fighting)

Each episode is named after one of the *Thirty-Six Stratagems*.

1. Remove the ladder when the enemy has ascended to the roof
2. Hide a knife behind a smile
3. Feign (pretend) madness but keep your balance
4. Slough (swamp) off the cicada's (insect) golden shell
5. Sacrifice the plum tree to preserve the peach tree
6. Besiege Wei to rescue Zhao
7. Defeat the enemy by capturing their chief
8. Leisurely await for the laboured
9. Create something from nothing
10. Kill with a borrowed knife
11. Loot a burning house
12. Deceive the heavens to cross the ocean
13. Replace the beams with rotten timbers
14. Obtain safe passage to conquer the State of Guo
15. Make a sound in the east, then strike in the west
16. The empty fort strategy
17. Let the enemy's own spy sow(plant) discord in the enemy camp
18. Deck the tree with false blossoms
19. Tossing out a brick to get a jade gem
20. Disturb the water and catch a fish
21. Sneak through the passage of Chencang
22. The beauty trap
23. Make the host and the guest exchange roles

24. Point at the mulberry tree while cursing the locust tree
25. Chain stratagems
26. Befriend a distant state while attacking a neighbour
27. Stomp the grass to scare the snake
28. Entice the tiger to leave its mountain lair
29. In order to capture, one must let loose
30. Borrow a corpse to resurrect the soul
31. Remove the firewood from under the pot
32. Take the opportunity to pilfer a goat 33 Shut the door to catch the thief
34. Inflict injury on oneself to win the enemy's trust
35. Watch the fires burning across the river
36. If all else fails, retreat

    http://www.zenpro.heychinese.com/sun-bin-art-of-war-36-strategies-7-dvd-cctv-p-215.html (Accessed on March 4, 2018).